Because we are ~~~
start, 'play' – th~~~
danger of being ~~~
toys and 'educ~~~
as if we are be~~~
childhood. Th~~~
balance. In order to write it, ~~~
first National Adviser to the Pre-School Playgroups Association and author of *The Playgroup
Movement* and *Living with a Toddler*, invited
parents to share with her memories of their own
childhood and of adult attitudes towards themselves as children.

Among the many aspects of a child's world
which Brenda Crowe describes and discusses are
the fear and comfort of darkness, children's sense
of right and wrong, of size, pattern and mathematics, the importance to them of repetition,
imitation and 'pretending', of imaginary friends,
'prized possessions' and 'working things out in
their heads'. Her exploration of the creative and
healing nature of play is continued when she
discusses how, as adults, we use play as a means
of testing our own reactions to the unfamiliar and
to relieve the tensions of everyday life.

Written first and foremost for parents and
couples about to become parents, this book will
be invaluable reading for anyone involved with
early education and child care (including playgroups, nurseries and mother and toddler clubs)
or with child development or preparation for
parenthood.

Also by Brenda Crowe

Living with a Toddler (Unwin Paperbacks)
The Playgroup Movement (Unwin Paperbacks)
Playgroup Activities (PPA)

With Kenneth Jameson

What's a House? (Galt)

PLAY IS
A FEELING
Brenda Crowe

London
UNWIN PAPERBACKS
Boston   Sydney

First published in Great Britain by George Allen & Unwin 1983
First published by Unwin Paperbacks 1984

UNWIN® PAPERBACKS
40 Museum Street, London WC1A 1LU, UK

Unwin Paperbacks
Park Lane, Hemel Hempstead, Herts HP2 4TE, UK

Allen & Unwin Inc.,
9 Winchester Terrace, Winchester, Mass 01890, USA

George Allen & Unwin Australia Pty Ltd,
8 Napier Street, North Sydney, NSW 2060, Australia

British Library Cataloguing in Publication Data

Crowe, Brenda
  Play is a feeling.
1. Play   2. Child psychology
I. Title
155.4'12   BF717
ISBN 0-04-649032 9

Printed in Great Britain by
Guernsey Press Co. Ltd., Guernsey, Channel Islands

Acknowledgements

I am grateful for the help and involvement of all who have shared their memories with me – in group discussions, in private conversations and in letters. Without them there would have been no book.

Sometimes I jotted notes while they were with me, but often I had to wait until I was on the train or in the car park before scribbling down all that I could remember. Tape recordings would have guaranteed accuracy, but waiting for the microphone and the formality of using it would have intruded and might have interfered with the spontaneity with which people spoke.

I have striven to record what I heard accurately and to retell it in the words and spirit in which it was said. If my recall or my retelling is in any way inaccurate, I apologise – and hope that, although occasional details may be wrong, I have always been true to the heart of the matter.

I am also grateful to Camilla Jessel for the sensitivity with which she photographed Edward in her kitchen for the cover illustration. He was a delight as he played up, played about, played to the camera, and finally lost himself in play. For over an hour he pulled, thumped, squeezed, stoked, poked and twisted a three-pound lump of dough. Once he reached for a small container of water, filled up the fingerholes and worked the mass to slimy smoothness – then to uncomfortable stickiness. This led to attempts to dry it up again with more flour. Then he thrust a large wooden spoon into the lump and, as it stood alone, exclaimed 'I've made a tree!' It wobbled and was reinforced at the base before he began to stick small pieces of dough along the handle, saying to himself 'It's a tree...and these are its leaves...country...country, we've been to the country...*country*...I've made a coun-tree!'

Eventually the play flagged and we helped him to clear away for lunch, Edward scrubbing the table meticulously with renewed concentration and energy. He ate three hearty helpings of cottage pie and two of ice cream, then suddenly stretched out on the settle saying 'I want to sleep'. Camilla has caught both the work and the happiness of that morning's play.

My deepest thanks also go to Vera Hughes, who not only did all the typing but swiftly became involved in the progress of the book.   B.C.

Contents

Chapter 1

'Playing!' or 'Nothing!'

On looking back down the years the two questions I can hear myself asking most often are 'Can I go and play?' and 'What's for dinner?'

Remembering dinners presents no problem: we lived on a farm and my mother was a magnificent country cook who made full use of everything in due season. I remember home-cured ham with sweet mustard pickles and jacket potatoes; steak and kidney pudding, the bottom suet crust heavy with thick, rich gravy, the top white and fluffy; rabbit pie and jugged hare, with dark winter greens and potatoes; farmyard hens steamed to tenderness, with parsley sauce; spring lamb, with mint sauce and redcurrant jelly from the preserve cupboard, new potatoes and early peas; Spotted Dick on wash days, sliced and fried in butter the next day, and sprinkled with brown sugar; fruit pies, filled with apples from the store room, raspberries, plums or black-currants from the Kilner jars; strawberries warm from the sun with cream skimmed from the pans in the dairy; and bread and cheese, eaten off a knife as the ploughmen ate it, under the walnut tree or in the dark warmth of the stables, with the horses tossing their heads in their nosebags.

The anticipation of dinner, the smells, flavours and feel of the different foods in my mouth stay with me still.

But what of the question 'Can I go and play?' I am in no doubt that this question held the same quality of urgent anticipation as my response to the dinner bell which called us in from wherever we were.

Our chairs had rexine seats, and our outgrown play clothes were very short. I remember the peculiar look and feel of bare flesh pulling away from the seat to which it had become stuck, for unless the seat and I were separated I couldn't slide over the edge until my heels reached the under-rail that gave me the leverage to break away and make a dash for it.

But where did I dash? And what did I do?

Much of the detail is hazy, but the *feeling* that accompanied the word 'play' has never left me. There are days when cooking a meal interrupts what I am doing and I resent the time it takes to prepare them. But there are others when I play in the kitchen all day long and go to bed fulfilled, with the restocked freezer as a bonus. When I am stuck with a problem, I either go and play in the garden or toy with a new recipe. Then the work becomes therapy, occupying my hands and eyes while the problem simmers in the haybox of my mind, sometimes resolving itself as if of its own accord in the early hours of the morning. Or I muse over the ironing board, daydreaming or playing with ideas, which rise like bubbles to the surface. And occasionally, when I am angry, the noise of the vacuum cleaner serves as a cover-up for a full-scale rehearsal of all I want to say to the object of my anger, only to reveal as often as not that beneath the superficial grievances lurks the real one I have refused to identify.

Real play springs from within us; and one of its many properties, at any age, is to help us to deal with stress. Many people discover this for themselves and derive great satisfaction, solace, refreshment from self-imposed jobs in the house, pottering in the garden, tinkering with the car. But if what we do is useful and has an end product we tend not to think of it as play. Similarly, we often fail to recognise the same work satisfaction that is such a vital part of childhood play.

Ironically, at a time when so many people are beginning to recognise the play element in 'self-chosen' adult work, others are trying to introduce the work element into children's self-chosen play out of a desire to hasten intellectual development.

If we break in uninvited to try to 'use' play for 'educational' purposes we defeat both nature's ends and our own; and, if we fail to offer children real play opportunities and try to create 'teaching situations' instead, we risk even greater harm for, as Rousseau put it, 'childhood has its own way of seeing, thinking and feeling, and nothing is more foolish than to try to substitute ours for theirs'.*

* Jean-Jacques Rousseau, *Emile*.

Years ago I used to ask groups of playgroup parents and teachers for their earliest play memories. But I stopped doing so, because the older ones so often replied defensively 'When we were children times were hard and we didn't have many toys', while the younger ones could recall many of their toys but often couldn't remember what they did with them.

So then I changed tactics and began to ask what they could remember about their first five years. Some remembered their first day at school, some couldn't remember anything before the age of seven or eight; very few other memories were recalled. This was worrying, for, if few of us responsible for children could remember what it felt like to be a child under five, how could we talk with authority about children's play needs?

Something seemed to have gone terribly wrong. I felt it was vital that we should find our way back again – not by denying the knowledge that research has given us but by trying to recognise when we ourselves are really playing and the feelings that play generates and resolves. For if we are aware that intrusion, however kindly and well meant, can shatter the intensity of adult privacy, concentration or enjoyment, then we may become better able to recognise when our children are lost in a private world of their own and refrain from intruding unless we have to.

I pondered all this for a long time. Then late one afternoon on a long train journey looking out at the lush green meadows I suddenly realised that I knew by the light and the length of the shadows exactly what the air would feel like out there, and the long grass against bare legs. Then another evening memory came back to me. My sister and I slept in a double bed, with a feather bolster between us because one or other of us kicked, though we never quite knew which of us it was. We would struggle to keep awake until my father had finished loading and roping the lorry reading for its journey to market. Eventually he came in so tired that sometimes he fell asleep on the bed as he told us our nightly snail story. But first he would ask:

'Well, what have you been doing today?'

If it had been a glorious day, whatever the weather, whatever we had done or not done, we only ever said one word:

'Playing.'

If it had been a hateful, rotten, beastly day, we still only said one word:

'Nothing.'

Suddenly I saw what a momentous question it was and just how much our answers meant. It was a revelation. The sum total of every single moment from waking up to going to bed had been 'play' if the day felt right in retrospect. Play wasn't something apart, it was life itself, a positive and creative way of living. If we had been bored, bad-tempered, frustrated and had come up against conflicts, still unresolved, then in spite of good food and possessions it had been a 'nothing' day.

Back I went to ever widening gatherings of playgroup people, social service advisers, teachers and other voluntary bodies and professionals working with under-5s and their parents.

Instead of my old questions I asked if any of them remembered a similar bedtime question.

'If so, what was your answer?'

Back it came loud and clear:

'Playing!'

'And if it had been a hateful, rotten, beastly day?'

Sometimes there was a slight pause, but then back it came, hesitantly at first, then triumphantly:

'Nothing ... Nothing!'

Once the ice had been broken by this common memory, the questions 'What do you remember about those "playing" days? What is your very earliest memory?' brought a much livelier reaction.

Usually people prefaced their recollections by saying 'I'm not sure whether I really remember it, or whether I've heard about it so many times that I am now convinced I remember it.' We can't always be sure about this, or that we haven't imagined an incident, or muddled memories together, or set an incident in the wrong time or place. But if it is real to us then it still has its own validity, either as family folklore or because our actions and reactions are often primed by our memories, no matter whether they are accurate or not.

Once freed from constraint, people began to respond more volubly – and one memory would spark off another one in someone else. What has been very noticeable is the number of times people have said 'I know just how she felt because . . . ' or 'When he was saying that I remembered how I felt when . . . '.

It isn't just what we do or what happens to us that we remember but how we felt about it, which is what really matters – for that is the truth to which we react.

The memories came in steadily from conferences and study days all over the country, and sometimes in private conversation or by letter after a meeting, and slowly I became aware that I was beginning to hear them in a different way. Whilst many were in tune with my own experience of children's ages and stages, others came together in unfamiliar groupings that made me aware of new dimensions in my understanding of children's play – and the more I thought I understood, the deeper the mystery at the heart of play became.

The memories triggered by the feel of the word 'playing' are often variations on recurring themes. Their recall can sometimes help put people in touch with their own forgotten feelings and create new bonds of understanding with their own children. It is for this reason that I would like to share some of the childhood memories I have collected and explore the questions they raise.

I know from experience that there are some for whom childhood was so bleak or horrific that they don't want any memories recalled. If that applies to you, you may be encouraged by the account of what happened to one such mother.

I was talking about early memories to a group of about a hundred playgroup people. All seemed to be well and one particular mother was sitting with a beatific smile on her face throughout – reliving a particularly happy childhood, I thought.

But she came up to me during the lunch break to say 'I want to thank you, and to apologise for not having heard a word you said after the first ten minutes.'

Her childhood had been hell. She was the eldest of five children, all of whom were seriously maltreated physically and emotionally. 'I was convinced', she said, 'that my mother had the other children deliberately to punish me, to make me look after them, which of course I did.'

She said she was listening to me at the beginning when suddenly something happened. She didn't just 'remember' something, she was so caught up in it that she felt she was actually reliving it.

'It was a bitterly cold day and I was shut out of the house as usual in a cotton frock and knickers and without shoes. But I didn't feel the cold, I was playing in a deep cart-rut puddle and I was totally absorbed in what I was doing. I could feel the soft mud squelching up between my toes and round my ankles, and there was a worm floating in the puddle. I had a stick and I could make it wiggle as I stirred the water, then I stirred it up too hard and lost it, and then I stopped and the mud settled and it came back again. I forgot everything except that. It was *wonderful*. I just sat and drifted and didn't want to come back.'

The feeling she was left with was that if there had been one such moment of perfect happiness there must have been others – and at last she felt free to let go without fear of what might come back to her.

After listening for years to adult memories of childhood it began to dawn on me that I had been mentally categorising them according to what are traditionally regarded as the various stages of child development – reinforcing rather than questioning my own received knowledge. But I didn't see this until I became aware that I was beginning to pick up a different set of clues, far more exciting because what I was learning seemed to come from a deeper level.

I was reminded of Wordsworth's feeling that children are born 'trailing clouds of glory' and of Jung's 'collective unconscious', which is, roughly speaking, the vast invisible wealth of experience, knowledge and creativity upon which we all continually draw, especially when we are very young.

But above all I was reminded of Dr Bronowski's certainty, which he stressed time and again during his *Ascent of Man* television programmes, that everything is linked; everything – music, art, mathematics, nature, man, past, present and future – arises out of and goes on in an unbroken chain, of which we are all a living part.

In this book I am trying to feel my way forward to a deeper understanding of children – and ourselves – by recording and reflecting upon my own early memories and those that have been shared with me.

The following four chapters contain flashes of recall that group themselves naturally and easily into the familiar framework of age and stage of development. I felt no desire to break away from this, for parents will recognise the stages of growth their children have gone through and some will be able to identify similar memories which will remind them that they, too, grew up in just the same way.

The next six chapters are a break with tradition, for although these memories could still be fitted into the usual framework of physical, intellectual, emotional and social development they obstinately refused to be so neatly categorised. As I continued to listen, instead of saying to myself 'My guess is that if she recalls her age it will be about three', I found myself thinking 'Another memory of darkness . . . not fear . . . not even the need to be alone . . . but of pure wonder.'

The reclassification of memories based on experiences came by stages. I have kept these chapters in the order in which they came into focus, for I am aware that their timing is linked to my own continuing growth and development. For example, the memories which form the basis of Chapters 9 and 10 have opened up new areas for thought coinciding with my deepening experience and observation of a whole range of patterns – particularly in relationships and behaviour – and the understanding that the more things seem to change the more fundamentally alike they are.

The remaining chapters were familiar ground but sharpened by memories that brought to life the difficulty children have in distinguishing reality from fantasy, the conflict between their perfectly natural needs and our conditioned attitudes, and the magnitude of the effort to become physically and emotionally independent from their parents – especially when parents are not always free from their own parents.

The further I departed from convention the more naturally things seemed to fall into place. It began to feel as though we were 'inside' children looking out, rather than 'outside' children measuring them against our charts or seeing them in the context of our homes and adult lives.

We seem hell-bent on robbing children of their childhood. That magic word 'play' is becoming associated with toys, or 'play situations' structured to encourage linguistic and intellectual development, and my heart goes out to the child who backed away from a wide choice of proffered toys and activities with the telling words 'I don't want to do any of those things – couldn't I just play?'

The time has come for us all to watch and listen to children more sensitively before we talk about them so knowledgeably. Children need *us* to recognise *their* natural feeling for play.

Chapter 2

Earliest Memories

Few people have clear memories that date back to the first year of their lives, but those who do are too numerous for the possibility of such early recall to be dismissed. Occasionally when I was talking to parents someone would volunteer such a memory, but more often a letter would come afterwards beginning with variations on the theme 'For no reason at all that I can think of, the other day I suddenly had a sort of flashback'.

The first came from Scotland and the writer said 'I suddenly had the sensation of lying in a pram looking up at yellow scented flowers against a blue sky.' This was so vivid and unaccountable that she asked her mother if it had any foundation in fact.

Her mother said that when she was about nine or ten months old they were staying in an old country house where the garden ended in a wood. Each morning the mother pushed the pram over the grass and turned it so that her daughter could see the azaleas; since they were wild azaleas they were scented. They hadn't been back to the house since, neither had the visit been talked about.

Another letter said 'I have a really vivid memory of water cascading down a sheer rock-face. It was black and gloomy and there were ferns growing by this water. They were not bright or large but nearly grey. Years later I asked my mother about this memory and she said that we only ever went near water like that during a holiday in Scotland when I was six months old and travelling in a cot. My memory seems to bear this out as I cannot recall seeing a top or a bottom to this fall.'

A third memory of the view from a pram or cot came from a mother who was brought up in a terrace house in London. She had had a sudden 'flashback' in which she felt herself to be in her pram looking at a pattern that filled the space framed by the hood. She told her mother about it and said 'It was like looking at a lace curtain, but it couldn't have been because I distinctly remember the hood was up because I could see the braid round the inside of it.' Her mother replied 'It *was* indoors, you know. Whenever it rained I used to push your pram into the front room and turn it facing the window – but why on earth did I put the hood up, I wonder. I always did.'

All these recalled experiences give the impression that the watchers were quietly and peacefully recording the scene rather like a camera taking a picture, except that one of them could associate the picture with a smell.

Others recall touch as part of the experience – 'My mother's appearance as a very slim and pretty dark-haired lady is very clear to me from an early age. I remember she always wore large beads and I used to finger them as she held me in her arms.'

I remember one of the pioneer nursery school teachers who, until her recent death in her eighties, still wore beautiful colours, with necklaces, earrings and brooches carefully chosen to tone, or match. She told me she did it after a child in her nursery said one day 'You've got new shoes!' At that time she was working in the slums of London in the dark days of the early thirties and she said 'I thought to myself that if they noticed new shoes I owed them something better to look at than the drab working clothes I wore each day. I've worn pretty colours and jewellery ever since – and they *loved* it! They used to come up to me each morning and say "What have you got today?" and touch everything.'

The first memories of some are associated with a feeling of fear. A twin wrote: 'I remember sitting at the end of a twin pram so I couldn't see the pusher – my paternal grandfather – and being *terrified* by a roaring thing emitting white smoke which whizzed underneath the road along which we were being pushed. The smell of steam trains always frightened me just a little, even when I began to travel in them to university at the age of eighteen. I know I was less than one year old when the incident happened because my father says it could only have happened during the months we were evacuated to Macclesfield and we went back to London before our first birthday, when the doodle-bugs started.'

A father had a similar memory of being in a pram when it was pushed under a dark bridge and a train thundered overhead. 'I can remember it now, it was dark and gloomy and then suddenly there was this roaring sound all round me – I was absolutely terrified.'

We have learned so much about our surroundings that it is difficult to imagine the first impact on a child of what are now our background noises. If we can be reminded, we may be able to anticipate some of the potentially fearful first-time experiences and allow the child in our care to observe them first from a manageable distance. If we are taken unawares, then at least we can comfort and reassure the child during and immediately after the experience. If we say 'Well, that's life, you can't molly-coddle them all the time', that's true, too. But there are so many unpleasant experiences ahead of them that it surely makes sense to make time in these early months and years to build up their confidence first in us, then through us, so that eventually they have confidence in themselves to deal with the unknown and the unexpected.

If we have difficulty in recognising or accepting a child's fear in a situation which we experience merely as slightly unpleasant but harmless, then how much more difficult it is to recognise the possibility of fear in surroundings that give us positive pleasure.

One mother told me 'I remember being pushed in a pram and left under the trees. I was terrified, they were tall and dark, and I used to scream and scream. I can remember now the peaceful feeling of being pushed in the pram – and then the fear as I discovered that I was going under the trees again.'

If babies could talk, this one might have said 'If you just leave the pram where I can see the trees but not be under them, I shall be quite happy and will be asleep in no time at all.'

There is so much guesswork in looking after a baby. Wonderfully quickly parents learn to interpret so many different cries – the hungry cry, the cry of pain, the overtired cry, and the cry of rage are all recognised almost from the moment of birth. Gradually we find we can tell the difference between cries which have physical causes and those which are an emotional reaction to us all-powerful parents, but perhaps we are less quick to recognise the very human cry of loneliness or fear.

Babies are people – and unless we credit them with feelings we may miss the connection between some of our painful adult states of mind and the small beginnings from which they grow.

Where does the depressing cycle of fears that is permanently part of some people's lives, and a recurring phase for many others, begin? Parents have more than enough worries and responsibilities without going into that question too deeply, but it is worth remembering that happiness is a state of mind which can be encouraged and that if something as simple as moving a pram a few yards one way or another makes the difference between a baby playing happily or crying in fear, then it is worth doing.

Parents need to be given confidence to trust themselves to learn from their own babies as well as from other sources. So often they allow their observation and intuition to be denied, only to discover that according to the latest research they were right after all.

Countless mothers must have said with delight 'She smiled at me, she recognised me!' only to be dashed by a confident 'That's not a smile, that's wind. Babies can't see properly until they are three months old.'

Now research has revealed that even a young baby can recognise a familiar face at a distance approximate to that between its own eyes and its mother's when it is sucking at her breast or feeding from a bottle cradled in the same position. Nature knew a thing or two, it seems, and, although part of the recognition may be bound up with smell, tone of voice and quality of touch, it all adds up to the fact that babies and mothers (or substitute mothers, for that matter) can 'know' each other very early on, if only they are given the opportunity to respond to each other as nature intended.

It is important that parents trust their intuitive feelings and don't allow them to be overridden by genuine or self-styled experts, for new ideas should be tested by all the people concerned, not imposed without question.

After each breakthrough on the research front attention is focused on popularising the central message, but often with little understanding of how it is likely to be received and acted upon by parents, especially the new parents of a first baby.

Some of the *communication* of recent and important research has been so unbalanced and insensitive that many parents have been given the impression that right from birth their babies must be talked to and stimulated non-stop. How exhausting for everyone that would be! Parenthood does not have to be that exhausting. On the contrary, although tiredness is certainly part of the early years, it is possible to discover a new serenity and wisdom through observation and heightened awareness – none of which can happen if the emphasis is on 'teaching' rather than on mutual learning.

We should also consider these 'musts' from the point of view of the babies. After all, they are the ones to whom it is all happening and they can't join in the general discussion. If they could, they might plead 'Must you make such heavy weather of it all? Couldn't we just be slow and happy together? Everything's new and strange for both of us.' With that in mind I would like to explore the idea that play isn't something apart, but a positive and creative way of living, an impulse that springs from within to meet each moment of opportunity and respond to it in such a way that we feel vitalised or calmed and enriched.

On a bad day hanging out the washing is a chore which does nothing for us at all. On a good day it is a positive pleasure to watch the clouds sail overhead as we wipe the line and peg the garments up in our own chosen order. I see hundreds of clothes-lines as I travel on trains and very few have washing pegged out in a haphazard way – the socks are in pairs, the underclothes, jumpers, trousers, sheets and pillowcases are grouped together, and sometimes I see a figure standing with the empty clothes basket on her hip watching the propped-up clothes flapping in the wind. She, and countless others of us, has taken the opportunity and a few extra minutes to do her work in the spirit of play, and will go back indoors refreshed to tackle the next job.

An old countrywoman I know speaks almost entirely in proverbs. One of her favourites is 'Well, improve each shining hour as they say ... ' With this in mind, there are two quite different ways of approaching the 'musts' that pressure so many anxious parents. Either we can use the time together to 'teach' our babies, in which case we may shine with virtue to the detriment of their harmonious development, or we can learn to take the opportunities offered, as they come, to enrich the quality of their lives and ours as well.

The first way places the emphasis on teaching, the second on mutual learning. The first is easier, the second slower and more gentle, though it may be more difficult for us in some respects. If we are prepared to learn from our babies and from our own feelings, we may discover that some of our deeply held 'musts' are clearly not right for our particular baby; nor, we may be shocked to realise, were they ever really right for us.

I sometimes wish I hadn't been brought up to feel responsible for everyone else's happiness, suppressing my own needs as being selfish. On the other hand, I am glad the pendulum wasn't swung to the other extreme, leading me to believe that I and my potential were of such importance that I was entitled to undermine the foundations of other people's potential in pursuit of my own, including our children's if they got in the way.

We are all our parents' children with all that that implies, but when we become the parents of a new child we are poised between two great learning stages in our lives, with a unique opportunity to question some of the musts and oughts to which we were subjected, while considering carefully the musts and oughts that are currently in circulation.

When it comes to bringing up our children, perhaps we should try not to think in terms of right or wrong, but rather in terms of 'This worked yesterday but it is not working today, so I'll try another way' or 'This works for me, but not for her' or 'This works all round, but my mother would have a fit' or 'This clearly works but I feel guilty – I hadn't realised that I was still so dependent on my mother's approval'.

In this spirit of inquiry, knowing that we have all built up a lifetime of habits many of which are routine and clock-based, try to put yourself in your baby's position. Take into consideration the possibility that the early flashes of recall experienced by so many people may be genuine, and that even if the parts of the brain concerned with conscious recall are incompletely developed it still just may be possible that babies have a way of knowing as yet unknown to us. Research is only the latest news, not the last word, and if we react to present findings with a healthy caution there may be less risk of overdeveloping one strand of learning at the expense of others about to come to light.

If you had just emerged from nine months in a warm, dark haven of water, with the rhythmic sound of a heartbeat and every movement cushioned, wouldn't you feel that being thrust into the world was a bit much?

Total apathy could endanger survival, but stimulation and repose are beautifully balanced by nature. When all goes well hunger or pain stimulates crying, which brings food and comfort, which in turn leads to peace and sleep.

According to my dictionary stimulation 'animates, makes more vigorous, or active, spurs on'; a stimulant is something (parents are the something in this context) that 'has a rousing effect'; and repose 'gives rest' or 'refreshes with rest'.

The alternation of stimulation and repose is needed throughout our lives, and if you have lost the art now is the time to restore the balance through rediscovering the real significance of play for yourself as well as your baby.

If you were loved, cuddled, rocked and talked to as a baby, and did the same to your dolls, toys or pets as you played, then these early patterns and feelings can be subconsciously recalled and re-played with your own baby. If you weren't so lucky don't worry – there must have been times when you saw other people loving and cuddling or stroking their babies or pets and you almost certainly copied them in your imitative and imaginative play. You still retain the patterns you stocked up for yourself. They will be enough to start with and as you learn how to play again you will help each other.

The stumbling-block is that 'playing with your baby' tends to suggest a parent endlessly tickling a tummy, shaking a rattle, or handing over a toy – all of which have a time and a place in the scheme of things. But there are intriguing earlier stages of play that are less easy to recognise. We may wince at scenes in romantic fiction where 'a smile played over her face', 'he looked at her playfully', 'laughter danced in her eyes', or 'he looked at her teasingly'. But like all clichés these have stayed in circulation because they express a recognisable truth.

Love-play between people of any age is the expression of feelings sparked by personal attraction and communicated through visual and verbal games and touch to the point where a relationship is made. If all goes well, this some-times leads to a union that may last a lifetime – and so it can be with parents and children.

Many parents fall in love with their babies on sight, but your baby may not have attracted you much, or even at all, in the early stages. Don't worry; think how often you have heard a happy couple say 'I thought he was horrible the first time we met', or 'I thought she was all right, but nothing more.' Give yourself time for love to grow, for only when you are happy and secure with each other will the musts and oughts fall into place quite naturally – and if they are not natural they will damage the relationship that means more to children than anything else.

Is it necessary to talk to children all the time?

Heaven forbid! There are times when we all need peace and quiet, a time to think, to live our own lives, to let go or just to be. Why shouldn't babies sometimes be left in peace? Waving hands or feet or contented noises coming from a cot or pram suggest that they are positively enjoying them-selves. Or they may be watching something intently, or just contentedly sucking a thumb in that lovely state between sleeping and waking. Peace and privacy are as necessary as stimulation and company – and allowances for both should be made at every age and stage, both for our children and for ourselves.

We should respect children's private playing time at every age. Sometimes parents worry about their children's enjoyment of their own company, or feel they ought to join in their play. But the ability to enjoy our own company as well as that of others is one of the signs of a well-rounded human being. If children are *positively* happy, then stand back until the moment comes when their concentration wavers or they positively want us. They'll let us know in one way or another. That is the time for talk.

If your parents talked to you when you were young and you talked to your pets and playthings long before you learned to hold conversations with friends, you will probably find you automatically murmur sweet nothings to your babies or talk to them as though they could understand every word. It is also likely that your voice will be quieter and slightly higher than usual, which babies love, and soon they try to answer with small experimental sounds of their own, to which you respond yet again.

These exchanges are a form of love-play that nourishes just as surely as food, which is why it is inadequate to refer to them merely as 'pre-language development', even though they are that as well.

But some parents come from families where no one speaks very much – and some, both men and women, are so shy that they can never think of anything to say to people anyway, and when they can they are so afraid that they are being silly, or boring, or will make fools of themselves, that they blush furiously and stammer to a halt. If this is you, don't worry. You have just produced an enthusiastic listener who will offer you limitless chances to play as nature intended – that is by trying out something (in this case, talking) again and again, in various ways and in a safe environment, until you feel confident enough to use the newly acquired skill whenever it is called for.

I once knew a mother who dreaded the period between her baby waking up and getting her safely started on the midday feed. One day, in desperation, she remembered a childhood game of playing at hostesses. Instead of going to the pram shaking with a lack of confidence which immediately communicated itself to the baby, she pretended she was going out to meet an honoured guest who had just arrived for lunch. Before she was quite in view she started to say 'Hello! How nice to see you. I've been looking forward to meeting you again. Would you like to come in?' She picked the baby up firmly and talked her way indoors. Inside, the role of guest and baby began to blur and she found herself saying in her hostess voice 'Shall I help you off with your coat? And would you like me to remove your wet nappy too?' It worked. It may have been her sudden resolve to be confident, or her calming voice, or coincidence, but since nothing succeeds like success she held on to her hostess game until she felt confident enough to talk to her baby quite naturally and easily as her ordinary self.

Fretful or bored babies often quieten if you put them over your shoulder and murmur close to their ears, or hold them in your arms so they see your lips moving as well as hear sounds. You may know what to say intuitively – but, if you are at a loss, try a conducted tour of the room. 'This is the clock that Uncle George gave us for a wedding present; we like Uncle George, he's big and fat and jolly', or 'Can you hear it ticking? tic-toc', or 'Its got numbers on it, one, two, three' – it doesn't matter what you say, so long as you know that 'one, two, three' isn't any more educational than good old Uncle George. You are talking to soothe, not to teach.

Again, you may find it easy to make casual conversation with people, but almost impossible to talk about your feelings and needs. Don't despair. You can learn by practising on your baby. As you bath, dress or cuddle, talking very slowly in a warm and gentle voice that may be at odds with your feelings, try saying 'Today is one of those days, I could burst into tears or shout at the drop of a hat, so I'm going to be kind to myself, and we'll take things very gently and get through the day bit by bit very slowly – even if things don't get done.' It is surprising how helpful it can be just to put feelings into words, and to hear yourself working out your own solution. When you talk let your words be bridges to friendship and the beginning of a lifelong relationship.

Do we have to stimulate babies all the time?

Again, heaven forbid! Commerce has been quick to respond to the undisputed fact that babies need stimulation and has produced everything you can possibly think of for babies to look at, touch, clutch, wave, rattle, bite and throw overboard, all to a very high standard of safety and much of it in hygienic plastic.

But the fact that we now know that even very young babies *can* see close to doesn't mean that they *have* to have things strung permanently across their prams. How sad if those azaleas against a blue sky, that sombre fall of dark water, or the intricate pattern of lace had been obliterated by a string of brightly coloured plastic elephants.

The really vital stimulation is still that which sparks between parent and child, leading both to become more aware of themselves as well as of each other.

Recently when I saw the mother of a beautiful and responsive five-month-old baby and commented on how much better she herself was looking, she said 'That's because I went to bed at eight o'clock last night and only had to feed Christopher once – I know now that I've been dead tired for ages, but somehow I didn't acknowledge it. Then yesterday when I was changing him I noticed that he was smiling and waving his hands, then going still, then starting again – and I suddenly realised what was the matter: my face was set in a frozen mask of weariness and he wasn't getting any response. I smiled at him and he nearly went wild with excitement, and then *I* was excited because I was sure he had been deliberately looking for my response, feeling puzzled by the lack of it, and trying frantically again to get it. So then we had a marvellous time. But if I hadn't noticed what was wrong I might have disappointed him for days on end until he gave up trying. What an awful thought!'

It *is* an awful thought, because that is exactly what can happen. But, fortunately for us all, babies go on trying in other ways, and at other times, and we gradually get better at noticing signals and learning how to respond to them.

What remains difficult is our own ability to adapt after a lifetime of trying to do the right thing, trying to be responsible, trying not to give in and trying not to be selfish. Christopher's mother had been so intent on meeting everyone else's needs that she hadn't acknowledged, even to herself, how tired she was – and even when she did it probably wouldn't have occurred to her to go to bed at eight if she hadn't been alone on that particular evening.

I remember another mother near to despair saying 'What can I do? I've got an eleven-month-old daughter who makes it impossible to put her nappy on because she kicks and wriggles. I'm not a fool, I'm a graduate, and I know I should be calm and patient – but I just want to slap her bottom hard. I'm doing my best to be quick and efficient so that I can put her back in her pram to play, and she won't co-operate.'

Somewhere along the line she had learned that play was important and had equated play with toys, especially 'educational' toys, of which she had an abundance. And she was finding it difficult to depart from her own line of thinking, and also to modify her own need to be in control all the time. She hadn't seen play as a spontaneous response to the moment – but her baby had. A cold, wet, soggy nappy had been removed, she was dry and powdered with a warm dry nappy underneath her, and she was making the most of her freedom to kick, stretch and flex her legs and wave her arms – in exactly the way nature intended, to stimulate her circulation and strengthen her muscles, through play, ready for the next stages of crawling and walking.

Sometimes nappy changes have to be quick, but quite often the only barrier to several minutes of valuable spontaneous play is our inability to stop taking the initiative all the time, to allow our babies to indicate the next step – for quite often their instinct is better than our set habits. And, who knows, this baby might grow up to say one day 'I remember my mother from a very early age. She had long hair that fell forward as she bent over me when I kicked on the floor, and she would put her hands for me to kick against' – and by then she may already have done the same for her own son or daughter.

Information about what babies can and can't see, how they 'see' what they see, and what they can and can't remember is almost non-existent compared with all that is glimpsed but not yet verified, and so much that lies as yet undreamed of beyond.

One of the fascinating things to conjecture is the stage at which words can be used to describe visual images and physical sensations that were retained without being understood at the time. Another is the extent to which we store up and pass on what we experienced as babies. Many of us know perfectly well that as older children we vowed and declared that we would *never* do or say some of the things that our parents did or said to us – and then we find ourselves replaying that record even to tone and volume!

Anyone who has worked with both normal and disturbed children knows the magic of real play to mediate between past experience and future alternatives. In following their play instincts children are helped to strengthen the bonds of love that sustain them, strengthen their muscles and reflexes, explore the world before them and their inner world of feelings, practise skills of all kinds, let off steam, reduce tension and replay uncomfortable episodes in their lives in different ways until the outcome is satisfying to them.

Through play we too can retell our version of an encounter that discomforted us, until finally we find the version in which we can convince ourselves that we came out of it with flying colours: not honest at one level perhaps, but the truth of the matter is that if we feel a total failure we may not risk a similar encounter, while if we have replayed it to our satisfaction we have both the courage and new learning behind us with which to face the future.

Play isn't just for children, for keeping them quiet and getting them on. Play is for all of us, helping us to go on making good the past and preparing for the future, helping to restore the balance between inner and outer tensions and pressures and, once the balance has been restored, making it possible for us to grow and develop in harmony with ourselves and others.

Chapter 3

Knowing without Words

Listening to people recall their earliest memories seemed to confirm something that emerged years earlier when I first began to listen intently to parents. Some would say 'I can see myself . . . ', while others would say 'I can feel myself . . . '. Thinking these might just be figures of speech, I began to question more closely: '*You* said you can see yourself, and *you* said you can feel yourself. Can you both explain that a little more fully?'

The answers were clear enough. There seem to be those who have the sensation of being back in time 'watching' the child they once were; and those who have no such sense of separation but say they seem to get back inside that child and see and feel it again from there.

I belong to the latter group and have two vivid memories. The one is of being lifted out of my high chair and in mid-air feeling a sensation of acute coldness as my top-half clothes were pushed up under my armpits by the lifting hands, and my wet nappy sagged uncomfortably downwards round my warm knees. The other is of sitting in a big pram, holding the end of the leather pram harness strap prior to putting it in my mouth. It was hard, pale and chewed into a misshapen stick quite unlike the rest of the smooth belt backed by white fleecy stuff. I knew that I was going to hate it when I first put it into my mouth, but that it had to be done because I wanted the next stage when it was soft, slimy, juicy, and immensely satisfying to bite on – and by that time the bitter taste would change to one that was pleasant. It is one particular occasion that I can recall, and I can feel myself holding the strap end in my white-mittened right hand and looking at it in this flash of 'knowing' as it was halfway to my mouth.

A senior adviser in the Inner London Education Authority has a similar memory which she described like this. 'My first memory is absolutely clear: I was being pushed in my pram, an old-fashioned high and deep one, looking over the side at the path which was slipping away backwards under the wheels, and I can remember quite distinctly knowing that I was going to remember that moment as long as I lived.'

Someone who was equally sure that she only 'saw' herself said 'It is like looking at someone else, I can see myself sitting on the floor behind the armchair in the corner. I'm holding something mechanical. I think it is a monkey on a stick or something like. I've no memory of doing it, but I know it is me.'

So little is known in this field that it isn't possible to make deductions. I just continue to note these differences with mounting interest, as I do the frequency with which people use their hands, arms and faces to describe their recollections and almost seem to recapture the essence of the recalled moment.

The mother who first alerted me to this said 'My first memory is of walking under the kitchen table and looking up' – she threw back her head and drew an arc above her with her hands and arms – 'and seeing this great big dark cavern above and all around me. . . .' A letter followed. 'Recently I asked my mother if we ever had a large old kitchen table. She said yes, when we were at Highworth there was a large old table in the kitchen and I always used to sit under it when I was a toddler.'

Another mother wrote: 'Most of my clearest memories are like *photographs* of rooms of relatives and friends my mother and grandmother took me to. My mother was amazed when I was able to describe accurately the old dark kitchen of an aunt we stayed with for a holiday. I was between eighteen months and two years yet I can still see the kitchen and its dresser with plates on end and the large basins along the top – so very high up.'

It is hardly surprising that most of the memories people have recalled from between the ages of one and two years have related to cots, beds or prams.

One middle-aged mother was hanging clean curtains in the spare bedroom when her teenage son wandered in for a chat. Suddenly he said 'Did I ever sleep in this room? And was the cot over in that corner by the bed? And did I climb over the top and fall in?' The answer to all those questions was yes.

When he was about eighteen months old – 'he was still in his Chilprufe sleepers with feet so he couldn't have been older' – he had a phase of waking up and crying during the night. Eventually the disruption to family sleep was so great that his mother decided to move into the spare bedroom for a few nights and have him with her. She put the drop-sided cot against the wall and her bed up tight against it, so that when he woke crying she could hold his hand through the bars for comfort.

One night she was too tired to wake until her son fell over the cot rail into her bed and clambered in beside her. The period in the spare room lasted only about ten days, and as far as the mother was aware there had never been a reference to the episode since.

This same mother can remember lying in her drop-sided cot quietly watching a daddy-long-legs hovering in the narrow space between the cot bars and the white rose-covered wallpaper. 'I can distinctly remember being very interested, but I also knew that I didn't want it to come through to my side of the bars.' We fell to wondering what her mother or father would have done if they had been there and she felt their presence would have spoiled something, but that if they had been there she would have wanted them to stand back and watch with her at a distance.

We mustn't allow the present emphasis on intellectual development to hurry us into breaking into such personal moments to name the object, or our parental anxieties or projected fears to lead us to remove or kill that same object if it is harmless. The moment is sufficient unto itself.

Children see something new one day – such as a daddy-long-legs – and then see it on the subsequent few occasions as though they were still seeing it for the first time. But slowly the repeated glimpses lead to the moment when it is *really* seen in a moment of great clarity and awareness.

We need to allow those first rehearsal looks to be peacefully untrammelled – so that the moment of revelation when it comes is as clear as it was for this particular child. If they are interested, children need more looking time than we can possibly imagine; so, when they are intent, we should let the moment hold them for as long as it will.

Sometimes a more complex fragment of time is re-captured, like the one described in this letter:

'This came back to me a few days after our session. Standing in my cot, which was end-on to my twin sister's, trying to heave a feather pillow, which seemed *enormous* though not heavy, up to the top of the rails so that my sister could pull the end of the pillow over to her cot. I think we were trying to make a bridge so one of us could climb into the other's cot. I remember feeling very relieved when our mother came in before we had managed it – I did not think the pillow would make a very firm bridge! This happened in the morning and I can picture the dun-coloured twilight room very clearly though not my sister in the other cot – I have a feeling that Mummy had rigged up some sort of a screen so we couldn't see each other, which would explain the need to climb over, I suppose! I remember most clearly trying to push the pillow *up* to the cot rails so I cannot have been very big.

'P.S. A general thing which again only occurred to me after our meeting. I cannot picture my sister in any of my childhood memories although I know we were together virtually every minute of our lives. I wonder what a psychiatrist would make of that!'

I don't find it difficult to believe that this mother could recapture not only the moment of doing but 'knowing' that she felt relief at being prevented. Many of us will have watched children 'feel' their way towards doing some-thing, even though they can't yet think it through and have neither the necessary knowledge nor the experience to accomplish it safely or satisfactorily.

I don't think we should mind too much about our ignorance in this field of the 'knowing' that defies descrip-tion, as long as we are conscious of just how much both we and our children have to learn. Once we can sense how much they don't know, how intelligent are some of the dangerous or apparently silly things that they try to do, how long it takes them to learn by trial and error and how hard they try, then it is easier to be patient, slow and consistent, as we try to guard their safety and our sanity under daily pressure, while also trying to learn how they learn.

As I have listened to people I have become aware that there is so much I thought I knew, in the sense that I could answer questions on a not very advanced examination paper, but reality had never suffused the words. I knew that babies don't know what is them and what is not-them: they have to learn that the hands waving in front of their eyes are their hands, but that the breast or bottle from which they suck is near them but not part of them. I accepted this and even passed it on, but it took a senior university lecturer to bring it to life for me when she said 'I can vividly recall my first conscious experience. It was waking to see my mother dusting the rail at the end of the bed. She stood with one hand on the brass rail and the other, with the duster in it, was on the big brass knob. She smiled at me and said "Hello!" I can remember my indignation, a feeling of "She's got up without me!" Then a feeling of total amazement that she was *able* to get up without me – I'm illegitimate so I always shared the bed with her. In fact until that moment I hadn't realized that we were separate. I was eighteen months old at the time.'

I have also become more aware of how intuitively wise children are during spontaneous play tailor-made uniquely for their needs, when they are under pressure that can't be contained or explained. I remember two examples of children coming face to face with the reality of separation from their parents, though in each case dearly loved grandparents had collected them for a short stay, for which they had been carefully prepared and to which they were looking forward.

The first example was told to me by a grandfather:

'When we got indoors Camilla became very quiet and went into each room to have a look. Then, with great purpose, she began to collect every cushion she could find and drag it into the hall. My wife and I unpacked and put the kettle on, and just kept an eye on her but stayed in the background. Some of the cushions were so heavy that she had to drag them, but eventually they were all piled up, and she climbed in the middle of them and burrowed down until she was in a little nest. She put her thumb in her mouth, shut her eyes and lay very still for quite a long time – then she opened her eyes, sat up, and came to join us for tea as though nothing had happened. From then on she was perfectly happy. But she had needed to find her own way of bridging the gap between home and us.'

A grandmother with a granddaughter of a different temperament a year older wrote:

'Dear little Katherine stayed with us recently for two days and nights – she was *so* excited about coming for "a very, very long holiday". On the way here she became very quiet and leaned on me, and when she arrived she was *so* pent up with mixed emotions. She didn't cry but everything that she looked forward to doing had to be done *at once*! "Grampy, get the slide out" and, before he'd finished, "I want to see Mary and James" (next door) ... "Want to paint ... go to the letterbox by myself ... no, with you ... do sticking ... get the bike out ...". It was as if the long holiday was now frightening, a long time to going back. We went along with her and in half an hour she was relaxing. It was most interesting, and touching, to watch her. We had a lovely two days, she really is a character! But when we took her home it was the same again – go here ... do that ... pick me up ... put me down ... and tears. But she soon calmed down and Jenny was gentle with her. Full circle?'

How (unnaturally) natural it would have been for the first grandparents to say 'No, don't play with the cushions. Come and have some tea. Look, we've got chocolate biscuits ...'. And how easy for the second grandparents to say 'Now don't play up, darling. We'll do all these things tomorrow. Let's have a nice tea first.'

We have so trivialised play and tried to confine it to the 'proper' time and place with 'proper' toys, or manipulated it for so-called educational ends, that we no longer see or recognise it as part of the life-force itself.

In every single recollection people have been quite clear that in the flashback to the episodes recalled they 'knew' what that moment was all about. How frustrating it must be for children who 'know' what they have to do to restore their balance and feel at peace again only to be thwarted by adults who try to divert them and jolly them along as though their inner experience had no meaning.

We must learn to respect children with the kind of respect that we were probably told was due to our elders and betters. I remember being told 'Watch and listen and don't answer back.' The same advice holds good towards children. But we can't expect miracles from ourselves after all the years in which various experts have questioned so many of our natural instincts, and materialism has eroded our deeper values.

We don't have to allow our children to do as they like all the time in the belief that it is somehow divinely inspired. We have all seen where that can lead! But there is a middle path if we can only find it.

Children's behaviour is perfectly capable of being manipulative, stubborn, vindictive, aggressive and altogether impossible. But that doesn't mean that the *child* is impossible, only that he or she is sending out signals to signify that all is not well. It is our job to try to decode the signals. In order to do this we have to watch what is happening and ask ourselves 'If that was me, and I could use words instead of actions, what would I *really* be trying to say?'

Sometimes children will be able to play themselves through to their own equilibrium, as Camilla and Katherine did – but for that to happen we have to be as sensitive and understanding as their grandparents were. We also need the sense of proportion that indicates when cushions have to be treated with respect and when more urgent needs have preference, and that's not easy.

But sometimes the message is 'I'm getting wound up and can feel myself losing control. Please stop me before I frighten myself any further – but stop *me*, don't stop *loving* me!' Sometimes it is a way of saying 'Your rotten old jobs always come first. Why doesn't my need to have your full friendly attention ever come first? The only time I know I can make you leave what you're doing is by doing something that makes you angry. I don't like it, but it's better than being told "Go and play with your toys" all the time.'

And sometimes what they are really saying is 'I know I've

got endless toys, but I haven't got anything really satisfying to do. I need real jobs, and legitimate messy play, and the sort of things that my imagination can get to grips with, and sometimes I want friends of my own age and my own choosing.'

Once we understand that behaviour can be a 'cry' it becomes easier to watch, listen, understand and respond to the messages that children aren't yet able to put into words.

Chapter 4

The Feel of Things

Once children spend less time in cots, beds and prams, and learn to walk so that they can reach much that they see, the world opens up like a giant oyster full of pearls. There are daily wonders to see, taste, smell, hear, touch, feel and do that no longer seem the first-time miracles they must once have been.

Because it is all so new and wonderful one thing leads to another as naturally as night follows day. Moral and social concepts of 'good' and 'bad' have no meaning yet. Parental disapproval is beginning to be connected with certain actions, but only if the parent and the temptation are equally strong and are present at one and the same time. When the parent is not there the temptation on its own is too strong to resist. But mostly children are not even aware of the pull that is temptation. It is all much more simple: 'good' is what looks, tastes, smells, sounds and feels good; and 'bad' is what makes you draw away.

One mother recalls 'doing good things' with touching innocence:

'One very vivid memory I can still feel. I was about three years old when I had a new pair of pale-blue leather shoes, with a strap fastened with a round button, like a bead. I remember the new feel on my feet and the sheer delight of wearing them.

'We had called in to see my grandmother one afternoon, and while the adults were talking inside I went out into the yard. Outside the back door stood the old wringer on its stand hidden under its cover, and beneath this a small galvanised bath with washing soaking in it. I instantly knew it was just right for paddling in my new special shoes. I remember the exhilarating feeling as I stepped into the cold slightly slimy water which spilled over the top of my shoes, soaking into my socks. Then the peculiar but blissful feeling of the squishing of water between my toes. I trod about on the clothes for some minutes, totally absorbed, until someone inside spotted me through the window.

'How surprised I was and how indignant I felt at the rude interruption, when I was hauled out and thoroughly ticked off.

'I could not understand at first why my mother was so upset and remember the feeling of humiliation in front of my young sister, grandmother and aunt.'

It must be so hard for children to understand that what seems so good to them can seem so bad to those they love. Children have to learn and parents are only human, but it is less humiliating if we can convey our distress about what has happened without conveying that we are angry with the child.

Another mother wrote: 'I remember filling my welly boots with puddle water and that wonderful squelching sound as I jumped. I can still feel the spray of water on my face as I stamped in the water and the cold clammy clothes as they got wetter and wetter!'

Some years ago I would have hazarded a guess that almost everyone had known what it feels like to be soaked to the skin; and how, once a certain unpleasant fairly wet stage has been passed, there is suddenly a feeling of being carefree – our shoes are squelching, the rain has penetrated our hair and is trickling down our scalp, there is no longer any point in being careful, and suddenly it can be exhilarating as we let go and splash on, meeting the rain full face.

Now, I think it may be rare. We moan about the rain (forgetting that our food supply depends on it), stay indoors, or protect ourselves with boots, raincoat and brolly if we have to go out. And I think we miss something vital, the link between weather and life itself. Children can love the rain – and wind, mist, snow, frost and sun as well – if our negative attitudes don't depress their natural play response of accepting and enjoying each day as it comes.

Many memories involve gratitude to adults for their understanding, whilst holding no malice for the many occasions when it wasn't in evidence.

An adult education tutor recalled as her first clear

memory 'I can remember standing with my hands cupped round a tomato that had just been given to me by someone – I don't know who. Father? Grandfather? – but we were standing on the path and he had just given it to me, and there it was sitting in my hands. I can see the colour, and the shape, and feel the heaviness in my hands now . . . and the *smell*! But more than anything else was the wonder and amazement that I had been given a *whole* tomato.'

Immediately someone in the group called out 'You make me feel awful! My son had his pocket money only yester-day, and he said that he wanted to buy a tomato with it, and I said "Don't be silly, you don't want a *tomato*!" And that was the end of that.'

We discussed it for quite a long time, because we so often impose our rigid ideas on our children without any reason other than our inability to keep an open mind to new ideas. Why shouldn't a child prefer a tomato to sweets? Above all, if he is only given small segments of tomato in a salad, or slices in a sandwich, or halves fried with bacon or gar-nishing a meal, why shouldn't he want the satisfaction of having a whole tomato all to himself? And be free to bite into it and discover that there is an art in eating one whole if you don't want to lose the juicy part with the seeds?

Colour is a source of great pleasure to children and they are particularly sensitive to the 'feel' that colours give them. One very vivid early memory was dated back to under three because of a house move. A grandmother had just moved for the second time, and her daughter said 'What happened to the lovely orange picture you used to have? It wasn't the last house, it was the one before. It used to hang *there*' – and she pointed to a spot to the left of the fireplace. The grandmother said she had no recollection of it at all, but as the contents of the last attic had been transferred to the new one she asked her grandson to go up and have a look among the stack of pictures to see if he could find one that answered the description. He came down carrying one, and his mother said 'That's it!' She told us that she knew it was the one because the familiar colour and the feeling of warmth came back to her as soon as she saw it – but she had never seen it as a picture before, and looked with interest to see that it was a cottage with a thatched roof glowing gold in the setting sun, with two figures talking at the gate, sunburned and dressed in warm browns and oranges, and a haywain in the distance bringing home golden hay against a sky streaked with sunset pinks and oranges.

Many people described favourite clothes and shoes, beginning 'It was a beautiful blue (or whatever) and I use to *love* wearing it.' Others have a different reason for remembering what they wore, like the young mother who said 'The only thing I remember doing is putting on something flimsy, taking off my shoes, and dancing all over the grass – it felt wonderful.'

The impact of size on children is something we tend to underestimate. A playgroup supervisor wrote: 'The one memory that springs instantly to mind is a clear visual one of my baby sister crawling towards me. She seemed huge, and I can still feel the thin coarse carpet we were on, and see the castors of our sofa. I have no idea why I should recall this memory as it is not accompanied by any excitement.' Others have recalled isolated flashes that were accompanied by quite strong feelings.

A father said 'I can remember a low hut or building of some sort in the garden, and there were lovely boxes of flowers on the roof. I wanted to see them properly, so I climbed up some stairs ... steps? ... ladder? ... to get them. I don't remember what I climbed, I just remember holding on and climbing up, and getting nearer. And then everybody shouted, and I was grabbed – and I don't remember any more.'

If children are involved in something perilous then yes, of course, we are apt to rush and grab, because our fear is so strong and sometimes our instantaneous self-blame, too. 'We shouldn't have left the ladder there, and if he's killed it will be my fault,' we say to ourselves.

The shock of it all is more likely to reinforce the message that ladders aren't for 2½-year-olds to climb than any explanation about heights, falls, hurts and dangers. But anger is often part of our own relief and it must be hard for a child to understand why people are so cross when what was done was so purposeful, intelligent, resourceful, and careful in the conscious holding on.

A senior educational psychologist distinctly remembers

being sick in bed, and then carefully covering his vomit up with the sheet. He can recall no emotion of fear, no desire for comfort, no feeling of revulsion that made him want to hide it – just the careful and deliberate act of covering up.

A playgroup tutor had a similarly vivid memory with no feeling attached to it. She saw herself 'standing up in a removal lorry beside my father, while the lorry went over a humped-back canal bridge'.

My publisher explored a memory from a different angle. He was born in Shrewsbury and lived there until just after his third birthday, and he said that he carried the clearest visual memory of the town for years. In fact, if any overseas visitors had asked him as a schoolboy for suggestions as to where to go to see an unspoilt historic market town, he would unhesitatingly have said 'Shrewsbury'. Years later, rummaging in a cupboard in his parents' house, he pulled out an old biscuit tin. 'It was the most extraordinary feeling looking at it – there was Shrewsbury exactly as I remembered it, with medieval houses and cobbled streets. What I had remembered all those years was not the actuality at all, but the picture on the tin lid.'

Some children have a particularly sensitive sense of smell. One mother had been surprised when she and her husband came back from an evening out to find her nightdress in their small daughter's bed. Her face was resting on it and one hand clutched it firmly. Next morning, when asked why she had fetched it and taken it to bed with her, the daughter gave the simple answer 'Because it smells of you.'

Several people remember dreading kissing certain relatives or friends because of their personal smell, and others recall the smell of certain cupboards, rooms or houses – sometimes with dislike and at other times with pleasure.

Three parents said that their children in this age group chose their library books by smell, sniffing among the low containers in which young children's books are often displayed in libraries, and picking out the ones that smelled right.

A grandfather with the clear recall of a childhood nearly eighty years past confided 'I used to get in the kennel with the old dog. I remember I used to crawl in head first, but then I couldn't see nothing so back I come, bum first! Then I turned meself round and backed in like an old hoss into the cart-shafts. I used to hide in there when I wanted to git away from 'em all – it weren't 'alf a tight squeeze. I can feel it now, the dog's soft belly right warm beside me, and the kennel hard on the other side. And the smell! Dear oh dear oh dear, that was an old spaniel that was, and she didn't 'alf smell.' Then he fell silent, shaking his head and withdrawn in reveries, until suddenly he snapped out of it and looked me straight in the eye to say with sudden insight 'No wonder I cut up rough when the old dog was put down, I remember I cried for days an' no one could do nuthin' with me. Poor old dog, we had some good times. But I remember that kennel.'

Many parents recalled their grandparents. One remembered walking down the garden path hand in hand with her grandfather to open his greenhouse. 'When we got there the windows were all grey and misty and I couldn't see in, which was funny, so I just stood still while Grandad unlocked the door. And then it happened, the door swung open and a rush of hot scented air was all around me, and the great big tomatoes shone red among the green leaves and I just stood there and it was the most wonderful moment of my whole life.' The impression it made was so deep that to this day it comes back to her every time she is on a train and whizzes past little houses with their tiny greenhouses at the end of the gardens.

Older people recall individual smells with relish – paraffin lamps, the carbolic soap in the kitchen, camphorated oil in the medicine chest, pickles being made, fresh chrysanthemums brought in from the allotment, sausage and mash and bacon, hardware shops with their smell of oil, candles, creosote and open boxes of nails, wash-days with hot soapy suds, stables, garages and breweries. And the memories bring back the 'feel' of the surroundings and relationships associated with each one.

But now there are extractor fans over cookers, furniture shines without the natural smell of beeswax and turpentine, aerosol sprays render rooms impersonal, deodorants perhaps make us impersonal too, modern roses are beautiful, but not many of them have the scent of the old-fashioned deep crimson velvety ones. New heavy-cropping tomatoes lack the scent and flavour of those that use to be grown for their flavour, school dinners are delivered in containers from far-away kitchens. Bread is pre-wrapped and few bakehouse smells waft out on hot air from shops these days – and even in homes there is often no time for home baking. So many distinctive smells that children could read like a book, connecting them with people, homes and seasons, have been removed or replaced by synthetics. The clock can't be put back. But it doesn't have to be accelerated – and, if we are aware of what is happening, we can exercise at least some degree of choice.

Taste figures least, possibly because we tend to avoid strong flavours for young children, yet almost everyone could remember the special flavour of face flannels, cuddly blankets, pram harness straps, coins, bread surreptitiously eaten as it was carried home ('Delicious!'), pencil ends, plasticine, uncooked pastry and various sorts of paper.

We've all done it. A perfectly natural part of our play was to put things in our mouth, and a perfectly natural part of our learning was discovering what tasted like what and whether we liked it. Sometimes we liked the feel but not the flavour, sometimes both, sometimes neither, and sometimes the flavour was harmless but the feel revolting – tripe and savoy cabbage still come into this category for me.

One memory, which formed part of a wider one, came in a letter beginning 'As a toddler I have happy memories of going to some very special parties. These were held by American airmen who were stationed nearby. They lavished all the love and attention on us that they must have missed giving to their own children who were left at home. We had puppet shows, fancy-dress competitions and, of course, lots of chocolate and bubble gum. As my substitute sweet ration was a chunk of cheese which was always munched sitting on a cushion by the fire, these new tastes were quite exciting. The pictures you may have seen of the Americans throwing gum and sweets to the children as they entered occupied countries have a very firm place in my memory.'

Sounds are nostalgic – 'the sawing of wood'; 'Dad

splitting the kindling'; 'the twin sounds of the pump handle being pumped and the water coughing up into the bucket'; 'the foghorns on the river'; 'the beating of eggs in the big white and yellow bowl'; 'the dog chain running through the ring on the kennel in the yard'; 'Mother's wedding ring clinking against the side of the pastry bowl'; 'the early morning clanking from the shunting yard'.

It is disturbing that so many of these sounds were recalled by the older generation; the younger generation has grown up with background music so easily available, and background traffic, too.

I begin to wonder if the need for background music also stems from fear of silence. If we never think, and muse, and ponder, or face our real feelings and what troubles us, or daydream and explore different aspects of ourselves, or just float free and enjoy those moments when it's good to be alive, how are we to learn to know ourselves and live with ourselves?

Children are naturally at home in silence. In fact they give every indication that they positively need it by withdrawing to be quiet when the need arises. Our son came in from the farm one day, dreamily peaceful, saying 'I've been listening to the quiet and it's full of noises.'

Only once in my life have I been aware of total silence, standing in an ancient olive grove in the deep heat of midday. Absolutely nothing broke the silence. Not a leaf stirred, not a bird sang, not a breath rustled a single leaf. Until that moment I hadn't realised how full of sounds our so-called silence is, but the sounds are fascinating if we would only listen. Try, just once, listening to yourself washing up, not just to the clatter of china but to the splashes drop and drips, moppings and sloppings, clinking, chinking and clonking.

Children hear the sounds that accompany what they do because they are *part* of what they do, as they slowly come to feel the rhythm of what they are doing. Watch them move astride a wheeled toy without pedals. Out of disorganised jerks comes a rhythm involving not only their legs swinging and pushing, but the counterbalance of their bodies swinging backwards and forwards.

Out of sound and rhythm come simple singsong words

and finger games, then songs with simple tunes (though singing in tune will take some of them years to master). This doesn't mean that they shouldn't hear other music, only that their personal experience and involvement needs to be encouraged alongside our own preferred listening.

A mother wrote: 'One memory of my childhood as far back as I can remember has been sparked off by my daughter's love of being sung to. My grandfather used to take me on his knee and sing two or three songs which I have always remembered. One of these songs I clearly remember giving a rendering of while standing on a chair in the middle of a garden party – in the days when children each did their party piece. I was about three. It is a time I remember with warmth. Now I have really without being conscious of it passed these songs on to my daughter, so how can people ever be forgotten?'

One day I was recalling the memory of sitting on the warm stone step outside the back door. The warmth penetrated my cotton frock and knickers and seemed to go right through me to be met by the warmth coming down from the brick wall through my shoulders – only the bricks were rough and little niggles of disappointment spoilt the warmth from that end. This memory sparked others, and a few days later a letter came. 'When you were talking about sitting on warm stone I was back on our slab of concrete outside the back door watching ants crawling up grass stems with the heat and the rough gritty surface against the backs of my legs.'

And another. 'Having my photo taken, the wetness of my little red knitted bathing-suit, the warmth and softness of the sand, and wishing the silly man would go away and let me enjoy it all.'

Memories of days at the seaside include the coldness of wet sand on bare feet, the hardness of sand ridges under the instep at low tide, the sting of sand wind-blown against bare legs, the warmth and softness of dry sand and how foot-aching it was to walk on, the strange sensation of standing by the water's edge and feeling the sand pulled away from under paddling heels, the abrasive sensation of wet sand being towelled off feet before the discomfort of forcing them into shoes – and the satisfaction when warm feet had dried the remaining sand and it could be tipped out into a little heap. And that is just about sand, which is only one part of a day by the sea.

Children have so much to discover through the endless little experiences that eventually come together to give a uniquely personal meaning to strings of words like 'a day at the seaside', 'shopping', 'read me a story', 'we'll catch a bus', 'pack the car', 'feed the animals' or 'time for bed'. And some words are so personal that no other will do. Grandma has no meaning for a child who has a Nana or a Bunnie Margie.

Words are only worth as much as personal experience has made them mean. Without meaning words are useless, but as I found everywhere experience without words can have both power and meaning at the deep level of 'knowing'.

It is later that words come into their own, when we want to make our needs known, share our findings and feelings, ask for information, deepen our relationships, pass on news and views, clarify and extend our thinking.

Words are connectors, but we mustn't allow the present emphasis on 'language' to blind us to the fact that children's senses cry out to be used *first* to provide the experiences that they will later need in order to connect. Children must feel the world, listen to it, see it, taste it, smell it, 'know' it, and us. That takes time and a great deal of silent investigation in peace and privacy

Children work so hard and urgently to know their world that, as I have watched them over the years, I have often felt some of them are further ahead in ways that matter than I am. They may need my knowledge, but I envy them their spontaneity, and so we have worked together.

'Life is indeed darkness save when there is urge,
And all urge is blind save when there is knowledge.
And all knowledge is vain save when there is work,
And all work is empty save when there is love.'*

* Kahlil Gibran, *The Prophet*.

Chapter 5

The World Begins to Open Up

In earliest childhood the self is the centre of its own universe, with a capacity for 'knowing' at variance with any real ability – as we understand it – to know almost anything about the immediate surroundings at all.

Then children begin to explore outwards, using their limbs and all their senses with a zestful abandon which often puts both them and our possessions at risk, and can be exhausting for those responsible for their care and safety. When you think how many falls and accidents children have, you might expect these childhood calamities to figure prominently in later memories, but they don't – and when they do it is the occasion that is remembered, not the pain.

Two fathers recalled such incidents:

'One of my unpleasant memories was the day I split my chin open on the back-door step. I can remember being bundled into a push-chair and taken round to the chemist for treatment – four stitches.'

'I remember my biggest under-five incident was cutting my knee very badly while playing football. I was rushed to the local hospital. "Rushed" in those days meant being dumped in an old push-chair and moving as fast as my mum's legs could go, as nobody owned a car and nobody had a phone.'

I remember falling on a doll when I was four. Her face broke and I can still distinctly see the broken head on the path, with the eyes on a wire stick. The doll was still in my arms and, getting up, I saw the triangular jag of china still attached to her neck, and blood pouring everywhere. I distinctly remember that nothing hurt, but my doll was broken which hurt unbearably – so I took her in to be mended.

I, too, was rushed in a pram to the surgery with a bath towel round my head and face, and it was interesting to see a spot of blood turning to a bigger patch – but nothing more.

A playgroup tutor had a similar experience. 'I remember that I trapped my thumb in the french window and I went running to my mother saying "Look at the blood – it's a lovely colour." I remember that she wrapped the injured thumb in a wet cloth and that wonderful dark red oozed through and looked so striking against the green cloth. I don't remember any pain, but I felt so cool and comfortable wearing that damp cloth on my thumb.'

Children cry with surprise or shock and, while we use the word 'hurt' thinking in terms of pain, they come to connect the word with comfort. If we overdo the sympathy they can quickly learn to say 'I've hurt myself!' as a certain way of obtaining comfort, whether they are in pain or not. Friendly interest, together with the fact that we register what has happened, is certainly in order, and there are times when 'Don't make a fuss' is out of order. But if we can keep our own emotion at bay we often discover that children don't always feel pain when we expect it – they may just need us to steady them against the surprise.

I wonder how often we project our own feelings on to our children, and how often we fail to understand some of the things that hurt them in other ways. Take, for example, this heartfelt memory. 'I was sent to nursery school when I was three – all connected no doubt with the war years and the fact that we lived in a basement flat. The memory that is really mine is bound up with a big brown cupboard – the shame of that cupboard! It was where the staff kept spare knickers for use after accidents. I can still recall the shame flooding over me when I had to go to the cupboard to collect a pair of pants because my mother hadn't put any on me. It was quite an honourable visit but it made no difference – in the eyes of the other children I wasn't a "big girl" after all.'

Yet a child of a different temperament, and perhaps with a mother under less pressure, reacted quite differently, as a playgroup supervisor reports. 'One neat and dainty little girl in our playgroup one day had an "accident" and her clothes were quietly changed and no fuss made. Thereafter, for some days, she wet herself and we could find no reason. Mum knew of nothing which could have upset her. It transpired that she just "liked Mrs Nichols's clothes"! She was loaned her favourite "set" and was wet no more.'

New babies in the home are an event for which parents prepare their first-born with all the care they can, but it isn't easy to tell what the outcome will be.

One four-year-old whose mother was going to have a baby was told how the seed had got in and where the baby was growing. She had felt it kicking and knew how it was going to get out when her mother went to hospital – and her parents 'knew that she knew because she could explain it all to other people'. But one day the home playgroup cat gave every indication that her kittens were going to be born during the morning, so she was put in a basket in an outhouse. Soon the first one arrived, clean and damp and perfect. A little later Betty took one of the children with her when she went to see how all was going, and they saw a second one born. The the four-year-old arrived, was told the news by the other children and asked if she could see the kittens. Betty took her with two others, and they watched the mother licking her kittens and purring. The farmer's son said confidently to the assembled company 'Our mare's just had a foal – mares always have foals, and ewes always have lambs, and cows always have calves, and then they lick them clean.'

At this moment the last kitten arrived, alive and well but rather messily, and the mother cat dutifully began to clean it up. The little four-year-old spun round to Betty, shocked and frightened, saying 'Is *that* being borned?' – and dashed out in distress.

Betty said afterwards 'I will never ever again assume that children know something just because they can tell me about it. I suddenly saw it from the child's point of view, and took her on my lap and explained about mothers being in nice beds and babies being bathed in warm water and dried on soft warm towels. It seemed to me that this was the cause of her distress rather than the birth itself.'

I doubt the wisdom of those who are beginning to

advocate that children as well as fathers should be present at the birth of a new baby. I don't think we understand enough about the visual and emotional impact on a child of seeing a mother in pain or drugged at one end whilst being delivered of a messy-looking baby at the other. Messiness, like beauty, is in the eye of the beholder and I suspect that a child could be deeply shocked by a reality that is so different from the imagined reality.

Two reactions to a new baby indicate the directness with which children see and hear – and interpret what they have been told. One wrote: 'I was four and a half when my brother was born and I remember going in the car with my father and elder brother and sister. I can see the drive curving up to the nursing home and Mother and a nurse coming down the steps. Mother was carrying a large bundle and I was sure she had lost her suitcase.'

The other wrote: 'As I was an only child I was spoiled in that all my aunts and uncles spent many hours with me. My uncles were bachelors, so I was given their undivided attention at all times. When my little sister arrived I was surprisingly pleased to greet her, as everyone thought I would be jealous. My mother told me that as I was her big sister I could teach her many things. She was born at home and, after she had been washed, weighed and fed and was safely tucked up in her pram, I thought that it wasn't too early to start teaching her all I knew. I rushed into the garden and pulled out a stick of rhubarb. With this tightly clutched in my hand, I waved it in front of her and whispered "Look, Linda, rhubarb." She smiled but I think that it was just wind.'

An indication of how differently adults and children view the same scene came from a mother who wrote: 'Another vivid memory is shooting across the road and scrambling up a high muddy bank, and balancing down and up a footpath pursued by my mother who was handicapped by a pram. And the lovely view from the top across a green rippling field to the railway embankment a quarter of a mile away which was so beautiful. Alas, it was all built over by the time I was four, and I can remember thinking how odd grown-ups were. I can remember my feelings of sadness as the muddy bank disappeared and a neat road with pavements replaced it. The building work was interesting but I was never allowed near to look. But I can remember my mother saying to my father "Thank goodness that's all finished." '

Another memory was of a secret joy carefully guarded, perhaps in the intuitive feeling that adults might not understand its importance. 'The drive to our house was covered with gravel. If you picked out the stones a large area of dust would be left. I remember tracing paths and roadways in this dust with my finger or a small stick. I would never put anything to represent cars or people on these tracks, it was the doing that mattered. Again and again I would trace out the paths with my finger, picking out all the stones and lumps and pushing the dust in ridges on either side of my pointing finger. When all was perfect I would then smooth all over with the flat of my hand and destroy all traces of what I had done. I even replaced the gravel.'

There have been lovely memories of family life, each with its own flavour:

'The main memory that springs to mind is when my mum used to clear up. She'd put all the chairs up on a very large mahogany table and we all climbed up and sat on our own bus, boat or train! We also used to put a blanket over the table and play indians in our tent.

'Being one of seven girls we played the game "houses", the older girls being Mummy and Daddy and us unfortunate younger ones being the babies. We had sticks or shoes or whatever in the layout of our house with gaps for doors; we suffered the tongue of "Mummy" if we just walked through the walls.

'To keep us quiet my mum would let us "cook". She used to set up a plank on two chairs and the twins and I would make pastry – each with our own set of spoons and cutters. I can remember the younger twin hammering currants into her pastry.'

And a father wrote:

'I don't really have that many memories of my life before school. I didn't go to a playgroup but I don't think there were many when I was small. I think my earliest memory was of my father taking me to the farm which he once owned. It was a typical farm with cows, sheep, horses, goats and a few vegetables. I spent a lot of time with my cousin and we used to go with our uncle to his allotment. The best part of this was the ride we would get in his large wooden wheelbarrow. Well, it seemed large at the time.'

A mother had particularly warm memories of her father:

'I remember very little of my early childhood but what does remain is quite vivid. Until I was four, or thereabouts, my parents ran an off-licence in Islington. My sister, being seven years older than me, was at school during early-day closing on Wednesdays. So this became "my time", when my father took me off to the pageant world of London. The ritual became quite fixed. The order of our progress I can no longer recall, but I know it included feeding the ducks in St James's Park, inspecting the "hair soldiers" at Whitehall and the "busbies" at Buckingham Palace, and always concluded with an ice cream and drink at the café at the Natural History Museum, whose location was somewhere behind the stuffed giraffe.

'To this day I retain some of my early conclusions that soldiers in mere khaki could not possibly be *real* soldiers.

'My passion for security also began at this age as my parents were very careful to impress on us the need for keeping doors locked and bolted to safeguard the contents of the shop. Their propaganda must have been very effective as I was well known for locking them out. I can still remember stretching up to close the bolts behind my mother as she crossed the road to a passing ice cream van. And my husband says I still check, at least twice, to make sure I have my keys before I go out.

'Stretching up is also concerned with my other main memory – shopping. I used to be entrusted with the ration book to go next door to the grocer for single items such as cheese, etc. His old-fashioned counter seemed so high up both to place the book and money and reach down the goods.

'I think I considered myself properly "grown up" when I could see over the counter in my parents' shop.'

This mother was able to trace her continuing obsession with locking up back to a training that was relevant to an off-licence shop, but sometimes we are burdened with childhood habits and attitudes which have no such sound foundation. It is another stage of growing up if, without any feeling of disloyalty to our parents, we can say to ourselves 'I don't need to do, say, think or be like that any more', and if we can avoid the trap of passing on outworn habits and attitudes to our own children.

Some grown-ups realise in retrospect that a parent who seemed rather frightening when they were young just 'finds it difficult to communicate with young children, but when they reach an age where they can participate with his interests he can relax and become great fun'.

Here is such a memory. 'My father was a very distant man to us children. He used to leave for work before I was awake and until I was five he used to return after I was put to bed. I only saw him at weekends. He used to do a great deal of work in the garden, which was over an acre in size. I would tag along behind him, but would make very sure that I was not too close. It was always a great privilege when he asked me to fetch something for him, or to carry a message to my mother. I would be a little fearful and be so careful to get the task right. Father was always the final arbiter in any matter, but looking back my mother never used him as a threat. She never said "Wait until your father gets home", but always "You must ask your father if you can do this."'

The need to do real work and carry really important messages is of crucial importance to children. They don't want to 'run along and play' if they can feel that they are important members of the working team that is 'the family'.

Many will be able to identify with this memory of being four. 'We never used to have a "Sunday roast", but the big family meal was always Saturday lunch. Father would carve and I was allowed to distribute the plates. I would carry them carefully to mother and then rush back for the next plate feeling full of importance and pride.'

These days divorce is so common that many will be able to feel for the child who recalled this:

'I cannot remember very much about my childhood but one event always stayed in my mind. I remember every Sunday after lunch my mother used to get me ready to see my father. My mother and father were divorced when I was quite young, and every Sunday I used to go out and have tea with him. If it was fine he used to take me to the park before we had tea. This happened regularly every Sunday until my mother married again and then it stopped. I remember I couldn't understand why at the time and I used to cry. But I suppose I must have got over it and my new father was very kind.

'Today I cannot even remember my real father but I sometimes think about him and wonder if he is alive and what he is doing, and what he would think of my two daughters if he could see them.'

Many of the memories from between three-plus and five years conveyed a wide 'feel' for the whole pattern of family life in which certain recurring incidents were sharply recalled. Here is an example: 'Before my mother bought her first washing-machine the washing was taken to the laundry in a brown board box that was fastened with webbing. I was always terrified to go up to the counter in that laundry because they had a large stuffed grizzly bear that reared up on its hind legs, snarling. I wasn't afraid of the animal, I think I rather liked it, but I was so afraid that it would fall on me and crush me – I was afraid that it would be so heavy that no one would be able to lift it and I would be stuck on the floor for ever and ever.'

At this age children's fears can be a mixture of fantasy and reality and although this fear was understandably real enough it was probably magnified by the child's feelings of smallness, inadequacy and helplessness.

Sometimes in their play children will create something as large as possible, a tower of bricks or cardboard cartons, perhaps, saying 'This is a great great big big monster, and I'm going to kill it!' – which is a way of reassuring themselves that they are not always at the mercy of everything big, that they too can be big, strong and effective.

One wartime memory is a tribute to the loving security that parents can and do create for children, even when they are under tremendous stress and strain themselves. 'I come from a large family, three brothers and four sisters, with mother and father – ten in all. At the outbreak of the war my older brothers and sisters were evacuated to Felixstowe, and my younger sister and I were at home with my mother (the youngest sister wasn't born until the end of the war). The air raids had just started, and with father away in the navy we all slept in Mum's big bed and the next-door neighbour promised to knock on the wall should we sleep through the siren. One particular night, my mother woke me up asking if Mr Stovell had knocked. I remember trying to listen for a knocking (I was three-and-a-half years old and my sister was eighteen months). I couldn't hear a thing. It was very dark and mother had a torch. She decided that we should go to the shelter in the garden, so she picked up my sister in a blanket and told me to follow her down the stairs. I can so vividly see myself with the "old gold" eiderdown draped over me and flowing behind me and mother with the torch and a sleepy bundle over her shoulder. I started down the stairs after my mother, but looked back to see my "cloak" flowing down the stairs after me.'

Other memories are a tribute to parents' understanding of human nature which they impart to their children from a very early age – one of the most valuable gifts we can give them. 'When I was about four I used to go to the farm with a can to get our daily pint of milk and I'd circle my arm and swing it round and round. One day the farmer's wife saw me do it and shouted "Janet, you'll sheet the milk!" and I did. She scolded me, but when I told Mum she didn't scold, she just said "Don't do it again when she is there." I asked why not, and she said "Because it upsets her."'

One problem parents face today is how to find a way of allowing children to do really responsible jobs. Many four-year-olds thought nothing of walking half a mile to the farmhouse for milk, or to the general store for groceries. They are still just as capable of doing such responsible jobs, but now busy roads often make it impossible.

Long before school age, children are able to scrub vegetables, even cutting big chunks into smaller ones with a blunt knife under unobtrusive supervision. They can make salads and fruit salads, rock buns, jam tarts; roll sausage meat into balls and make the batter for toad-in-the-hole; clean shoes, copper, brass and silver; scrub the doorstep, the number plates of the car, the draining board and the washing-up bowl; wash dolls' clothes and small items of the family wash. Even if you have a washing-machine children need to learn how to wash clothes – 'in case', as my mother would say.

Hand in hand with their unsuspected abilities goes their lack of knowledge of such adult concepts as, for example, perspective – for childhood has its own specific areas of 'not knowing' as well as 'knowing'. One mother said 'I was brought up in care in a convent and one day I was upstairs looking out of the window. Down below, right at the end of the grounds, they were getting ready for a fête or a pageant or something – I don't know what it was – but there was the most beautiful row of flags fluttering on little sticks. They were *so* pretty. I rushed downstairs and outside as fast as I could go. I knew exactly what I wanted to do, I wanted to pick a bunch of them. I ran and ran and ran – and then I looked up, and they had grown as tall as a house, and I couldn't pick them at all.'

Toys figured hardly at all in the memories people shared, perhaps because real play is so often without bought toys, unless they are a means to an imaginative end – such as little cars, dolls, soldier dolls, bricks, push-and-pull and ride-on toys or construction toys. But one father said 'I do remember my first box of paints. It was a large box with soldiers on the lid. And of course I remember my first bike. I must have been four at the time. It was a large three-wheeler and it was painted red and blue I was seldom seen doing anything else but riding my bike.'

Dressing up was remembered with enthusiasm for the sheer fun of it. One mother wrote: 'I remember dressing up in Mum's wedding shoes and really believing they were made of gold. Putting on her treasured fox fur when she wasn't looking, even though I was in fact terrified of the thing. And falling downstairs as a result of the wedding shoes – how that hard bristly mat on which I landed hurt!'

We mustn't overlook children's response to anything beautiful or interesting, which they see and 'feel' quite objectively: a picture hat smothered in artificial flowers, a trilby, a fur hat, a sequined jacket, a frilly dress or a shawl – in a child's eyes quite unlinked with sex. It is perfectly natural for both boys and girls to want to try on everything, and to enjoy the unaccustomed image that greets them in the looking glass.

It is also perfectly natural for both boys and girls to want to dress up in order to play at being their mother or father (or whoever it is who looks after them for most of every day). This, of course, has nothing to do with transvestite tendencies, but everything to do with trying to find out how it feels to be the sort of person who says 'Go and wash, you're not going to eat with hands like that' or 'There, there, it's all right, we'll put a sticking plaster on it' or 'I've told you a thousand times, *shut that door!*' or 'We've got to go out . . . put on your coat . . . where's my purse? . . . now hurry up.' It is also necessary sometimes for them to control smaller children or dolls as a way of escape from the feeling that they are always under authority and never in charge.

Children need to know where parents draw the line, and to feel that they have to be careful not to cross certain barriers. They need to feel useful and important, doing adult jobs on equal terms whenever possible; they need messy play and imaginative play as well as playing with toys and playing about; they are bound to make mistakes and to 'give in to temptation'. We owe it to them to be understanding and forgiving as often as possible, so that when we do (inevitably) behave insensitively or unjustly they can forgive us as generously as we have forgiven them.

Now we have been made so aware of the need to stimulate children it is time also to be aware that stimulation isn't necessarily something that has to be done by us, to them. Ordinary everyday living provides continual possibilities – but it is we who create the atmosphere and relationship which encourages children to notice and respond to everything and everyone about them, or to draw back or to be blunted into apathy.

If we feel the responsibility is entirely ours we may stimulate them according to *our* perception of colour, sound, taste, smell, touch and feelings. That would be sad, for their spontaneous interest, enjoyment and zest for living is so vivid. And ours is often so blunted by familiarity, tiredness or lack of confidence to trust our own first-hand feelings instead of relying on those handed down to us from birth onwards.

Chapter 6

The Fear and Comfort of Darkness

Fear of the dark is so widespread that it is sometimes thought to be natural or instinctive, like fear of loud noises or fear of being dropped. In fact it isn't, but other fears come to be associated with it, and other people communicate their own fear, so children often begin to acquire a fear of the dark from sources other than their own experience of it.

Some people are uncomfortably familiar with the particular kind of fear which we call depression, others are only afraid when there is a logical reason, and yet others are either so well adjusted or so lacking in imagination that they can no longer recall whether they were afraid as children and, if so, of what, and how it felt. If we are to help children to outgrow their fears, we need be aware of how they actually feel when they are afraid.

In trying to learn more about children's fears I asked a teacher with a class of thirteen- to fourteen-year-old boys if she would ask them to complete the sentence 'When I am frightened I feel . . .'. These are some of the answers:

'As if I can faint'; 'I feel panicy and feel I have to run away from something'; 'I feel very faint and my head spinds and I run anyware'; 'I feel panicy and between sad and happy'; 'I feel scared and panic and rush about'; 'I feel shaky and tense and I can feel my blood running round my body'; 'I feel helpless'; 'I feel stupid and unhappy'; 'My body sinks inside me'; 'I feel very sad'; 'I feel all knumb and I feel stupid'; 'I feel like I would cry'; 'I feel mad'; 'My stomach feels heavy and I get a tingle in my testicles'; 'I feel nerves and I am also thinking about the exam I had. My hands always swats a lot.'

These boys knew fear all right and I was glad to be reminded of the physical impact of fear, for I knew it as a child but with the passing of the years the actual physical memory of fear grows hazy, and it becomes all too easy to refer to 'children's little fears and fancies'.

Fear of the dark figured prominently in early memories, but it wasn't until people began to pinpoint precisely which dark places they feared that real sensations of fear were recalled. The superficial comment 'I used to be frightened of the dark' does nothing to connect us with frightened children. Without this living link of experience it is difficult to know how to comfort children, and then how to help them in *their* time and way to overcome and finally outgrow their fears. Above all, we may fail to see how often they use play to help themselves – or could if we didn't unwittingly prevent it happening.

Among the specific fears of dark places were the following:

'I can remember being afraid to go in the potting shed alone, it had a tiny window covered in cobwebs so it wasn't completely dark, but if you went in out of the sunshine it was quite dark for a minute – and then it was horrid. Things standing around, bundles of pea-sticks all spikey, sacks, piles of pots, the tools in racks, the lawn-mower looking huge. Everything smelt different, sackish and flowerpottish and dusty, and it was so quiet and still. I used to think something would jump out at me, and if I touched something – like getting a pot or a stick – everything else would move and I thought it was all going to fall on top of me.'

'I used to hate going upstairs when it was light in the hall, it felt like walking out of safety into danger – we couldn't turn the landing light on till we got upstairs, and I used to dread reaching up to find the switch. And then when it was light I felt the same again about the dark bedrooms.'

'I was so frightened that there was something under the bed that I didn't dare look, and I couldn't go to sleep because I hadn't looked. If Mum came up I'd call out and say "Can you look under the bed? I've lost my hankie", and she'd say, "No, it's not there – here, have mine." I've often wondered if she knew. She must have done because it happened so often.'

Good for Mum, she recognised that her child was trying to cope with the fear by herself in her own way, and gave her the reassurance she needed without causing her to lose face.

Others weren't bothered about what skulked under the bed; it was between the sheets that danger lurked. Some would strip the covers right back to inspect the bed before getting in, other thrust their toes down to the bottom while they were having their goodnight kiss – in the reasonable assumption that if there was anything there parental arms would pull them to safety in a flash. Some worked their feet down inch by inch, and others turned round and made the inspection head first with hands finding the way and bottom in the air to widen the gap between the sheets.

Several could remember the fear that something nameless would grab their ankles from behind and below as they went upstairs: they invented their own systems of lifting their feet very fast and high, or jumping from one side of the stairs to the other, or giving a kick back before lifting that foot quickly on to the next stair.

All these games are ways in which children spontaneously use play to overcome their fears and build up their self-confidence. If we understand this we can watch their courage and efforts to help themselves with respect, and won't be tempted to say 'What on earth are you doing? Walk upstairs properly.'

Shadows were another source of fear, especially if they moved. Some could remember individual rooms very clearly. 'We had a street lamp outside and it used to throw the pattern of the lace curtains on to the wall and ceiling. Mum always opened the window at the top and if the wind got up the curtains blew and the shadows darted about. I didn't understand any of this of course, I just used to see these awful dark shapes coming for me. I was terrified.'

Another memory concerned curtains. 'In the daytime my bedroom curtains were lovely, covered with huge flowers, but at night when they were drawn and the street light shone behind them the flowers looked like tigers' faces – every time the curtains moved I thought they were going to pounce on me. I couldn't bear to look at them, and I didn't dare turn my back to them – I used to huddle under the covers and hope that if I couldn't see them they couldn't see me.'

There are several reasons why these fears are so vivid. Children have wonderfully creative imaginations, and in the early years fact and fantasy have no clear boundaries. Flowers *could* change into tigers, and curtain-tigers *could* jump on the bed. In much the same way we may look at a glossy magazine, be riveted by an eight-stone five-foot-ten model and 'see' our eleven-stone five-foot-three selves looking just like that if only we could find an identical dress.

Children's fantasies are made more real still because children don't yet have enough experience or knowledge to know about shadows and tigers – whereas ours are made more real by the fact that sometimes we don't want to see ourselves as we really are, or because we haven't yet discovered who we really are and so 'play' with various images of ourselves to help us discover our true selves.

Sometimes the fears can be explained away if the children are able to put them into words, or if we have enough imagination to guess what they are thinking and have the presence of mind to say 'Can you see things on the wall? When I was your age I used to be frightened, too, until I knew what made them. Look, I'll show you' – and then explain about the light outside and the pattern on the curtain. The light can be turned out and the curtain held still while the child looks at the dreaded pattern on the wall and ceiling, and when we say 'Now I'll shake it and make the patterns move' they can see it happen. If this is done once or twice the child may be ready to hop out of bed and help with the shaking. Then you can lie on the bed while the child make the shadows move.

Fears don't usually fade until we feel we have a degree of control over what is frightening us – but that alone is not enough. There are times when knowledge and intelligence tell us there is absolutely nothing to be afraid of, but our emotional state refuses to accept the message – and we panic regardless. This is particularly so in parenthood, because we are emotionally involved with our children. A cold is pneumonia and it's our fault; he's late coming home from school, he must have had an accident; she's wildly in love, and he'll let her down. On and on it goes. And if we are honest about how real our fears are to us we can better understand how real children's fears are to them.

Fears can't be overcome with force, and if they are repressed inner stress will surface again in physical symptoms or a new fear that takes the place of the old one. If a child is afraid of the dark it is both unkind and pointless to insist that the landing light must be turned off 'because we're not having this sort of nonsense' or 'because you're old enough now not to be afraid of the dark'.

It doesn't make children brave to deny them a helping hand, any more than it makes them brave if they come to rely totally on parents to keep them safe without having to do anything about it for themselves. We need to help them accept their fears as natural for their age *or stage*, for we all regress from time to time and a child who was once happy to sleep in the dark may go through a bad patch when he needs a light again for comfort as he struggles to cope with whatever it is that has temporarily set him back. They also need us to offer them hope – 'It's all right, lots of people feel like you, and one day you will suddenly find that you don't need the light any more – perhaps after your next birthday, or the one after that.' Don't set the target too near or it will be an added anxiety.

But not everyone I spoke to remembered darkness with fear. Some had lovely memories of night quite unconnected with darkness. One remembered a magic night of snow, starlight and the moon, when she was taken out with uncles and aunts and they went tobogganing down a hill. Muffled up and held close she felt she was flying past the clumps of trees for ever and ever. And she can still hear the sound of the runners on the snow and see the frozen lake below where tiny people were moving about in patterns. Everyone was laughing and calling out and she had never seen or heard parents and relations like this before – or since. This one night of enchantment comes back to her each time the night sky is high and clear and the air has a nip of frost.

Another memory, from an actress, is of being held in her mother's arms, wrapped about in a shawl, at an open bedroom window. Her mother said 'Look at the moon!' and she remembers both looking at the huge silent silvery moon and being aware of the way her mother was looking at it too.

Both men and women remembered making houses under the bedclothes, especially those who shared a double bed. Pillows and bolsters were made into walls down the middle, or across the bed halfway down. For some unknown reason it was quite hard to make the first move down, but once under there seemed to be all the room in the world and movement was perfectly easy – but different and hilarious. And then parents would call 'What's going on up there? Be quiet and go to sleep.'

In each group where these memories were shared I asked if their children did the same thing. Most of them did. And what was the response? 'What's going on up there? Be quiet and go to sleep'! But why? It was all so harmless and such fun and we went to sleep eventually, not because we were told to but because sleep overcame us.

It's strange how we store up our parents' reactions and even whole chunks of their dialogue, and then adopt them as our own when the time comes to identify with the parental role. Why don't we hold on to our childhood memories as well? Then sometimes we could be on our children's side and leave them alone to enjoy what we once enjoyed.

Other memories centred on the longing for privacy, and darkness was felt to be a part of privacy.

I can remember the cupboard by the kitchen range where I used to hide on a pile of newspapers uncomfortably gritty with dust and crumbling plaster. The flat irons and trivets lived in there, and the box containing blacklead polish for the grate and blocks of coarse whitening for the hearth. All these things had their own separate smells, which mingled to give the cupboard a particular smell of its own, which was enhanced by the warmth of the range.

It was a relief to opt out for a while, to feel you couldn't be got at, to be hidden and confined in a small warm dark space before feeling ready to break out into the world to get on with living once more. It was a strange feeling to watch other people getting on with their jobs, and even stranger still to hear them talking together. It wasn't a bit like being in the same room listening to them. They seemed so ordinary and impersonal, and I can remember the importance of that distancing.

All those who remembered hiding in cupboards could describe their particular cupboard in detail, and all remembered the relief of opting out. But one recalled other feelings, too:

'When it was raining or it was too cold to go outside I used to climb up into the airing cupboard. This reached up to the ceiling and so had shelves above the hot tank. The topmost shelf housed the sleeping bags and this is where I used to snuggle up – so warm and so safe. My family never knew where I was, and I remember that queer feeling of power when mother would call and call for me and couldn't find me. I would climb down only when I was certain that there was no one about, and that included my brothers and sister.'

Children need access to somewhere private occasionally, even if it is only under the bed or a table. The pace of living increases all the time, and adults are so large and powerful and – let's face it – bossy for so much of the time. The words 'Hurry up, come along, be quick' are habits of speech that don't matter much to us when we are grown up. But they do to a child who finds tasks like putting the right arm into the right coat sleeve or matching the right button to the right buttonhole immensely complicated and demanding. How would you feel if someone stood over you while you changed a wheel on the car or wrote an important letter saying 'Hurry up, come along, be quick'?

Let them opt out – and, if there is no other space for them, throw a blanket over a table and let that be a private retreat.

The need to see without being seen is another facet of the need for privacy, which comes through clearly in one letter:

'My tree was too simple and close to the ground for my brother and sister to climb so it was all mine. I remember being so certain that if I could not see anyone it followed that no one could see me. My tree was fairly close to the road so if I sat in the higher branches I could see the forbidden traffic. If I stood on the gate that led to the road I was very close to the sanctuary of my tree and if anyone came I could run under the leaves and no one ever saw me. I dug to Australia under that tree. It took me weeks, and the hole never got deeper than my knees, but I was so sure that I would reach Australia tomorrow. When a neighbouring fir-tree crashed to the ground that winter it missed my tree by inches and I remember the intensity of my relief that my tree was still there. When my father sawed the fallen tree into logs it was a very long weekend. My tree was not my own any longer. People stood around it and it was so noisy.'

One other form of privacy all children should have is a private place to keep special treasures, small enough to carry about with them if necessary. A tiny suitcase or a plastic picnic case with the contents transferred to a little basket make a satisfying birthday or Christmas present – which doubly guarantees that it is special. Later on a slightly larger suitcase or a wooden tuck-box with its own lock and key (tied with scarlet ribbon to make it less easy to lose, with the spare key in your own private place) ensures that there are some things which never have to be shared or given even temporarily to a younger brother or sister with the unfair pressure of 'Give it to her, she's only a baby'. Would you want to lend your engagement ring to someone – even your 'baby sister' – just because she wanted to borrow it?

A closed box, drawer or cupboard gives a pleasing sense of security and there is something about darkness that makes it particularly satisfying for hiding things away. We all need to keep a part of us to ourselves, even within the context of marriage or friendship, and this is as true for children as it is for us. And whatever our age we have to work out for ourselves what stays apart and what is shared. Exactly what will change with the years, but children can't think as we can and until they are older may not be able to distinguish between guilty-hiding, fun-hiding, precious-hiding and just hiding-hiding – or if they do their idea of 'fun' or 'precious' is not always ours.

Something that locks up and is unconditionally theirs helps them to begin working out the difference in a simple practical way – but keep an eye on the hamster.

Chapter 7

Bliss

When I ask groups of parents what they most want for their children the immediate answer is *always* 'happiness' or 'health and happiness'. The question 'And if you can only choose one?' invariably brings them back to happiness, but not until they have talked it through and come to the conclusion that a great many people seem to have health without happiness.

Since this quality of happiness is so difficult to define – and the dictionary definition, 'contented or pleased with one's lot', isn't what all of them are after – I ask people to describe how they feel when they are happy by their own definition – they can always recognise happiness when it arrives.

These are some of the things they say. 'I feel tall and light'; 'It bubbles up inside and you want to smile'; 'Nothing is any trouble, the day just flows along'; 'You wouldn't change places with anyone'; 'You love everyone and everything, and everyone you meet is nice because it's catching'; 'It makes you want to hold on to it because you know it can't last'; 'Real happiness isn't the same as having a nice time, at a party or buying a new dress – though that's nice too'; 'When I'm happy I wander over the house when everybody's out, and just say "Hello" to it all, and think how lucky I am'; 'It's a feeling of being right with yourself'; 'It's being peaceful deep down, so that even when things go wrong on the surface and it's hard to cope with it all you know that underneath it's still all right'; 'It's not needing to please other people all the time, it's feeling that it's all right to be *you*'; 'You feel you've got there and can take a breather – only you discover there are more valleys and more mountains ahead. When I'm going down I lose it, but then I climb out and can look back and see that I've just learned something – then happiness comes back and I go on for a long time before the whole learning cycle happens again'; 'Happiness is satisfaction, I don't think anybody could be happy who didn't *do* something – I don't necessarily mean an outside paid job, I feel happy when I've had a good day with the children, or when I've turned out a room, or filled up the freezer'; 'Happiness is doing nothing, just lying on hot sand listening to the sea, and knowing that you haven't got to do anything – bliss!'

Children have a wonderful capacity for happiness though they vary in the way it is expressed. Some are born with a happy temperament and remain sunny all their lives; some babies find it hard to adapt to life outside the womb and take months to settle into a more peaceful way of life, but that doesn't mean they are 'born miserable'; some are outgoing and boisterously happy, while others are quietly happy.

Happiness is caught rather than taught, but fundamentally it comes from within as a by-product of living in harmony with oneself, with others, and in the world – which is why it is so important to understand that play is the spontaneous force that regulates the balance between feeling happy and satisfied and feeling bottled up inside, pressured from outside and out of harmony with everything and everyone.

Parents know themselves and their children well enough to recognise what happens when sweets are bought at the check-out till to keep the peace under pressure. Finally getting them gives 'got what I wanted' satisfaction; there is also the pleasure of anticipation as they are unwrapped, and the brief pleasure of eating them. But none of that adds up to happiness.

Many of the earlier examples described deeply satisfying pleasures through the senses that did add up to happiness, and some of them owed a great deal to the people who were there at the time. But every now and then someone would use the word 'bliss' to indicate a special moment, or would write about a memory in such a way that bliss didn't seem an exaggeration – these accounts conveyed the feeling of children who felt cherished, important and safe in every sense of the word, and whatever was happening was being savoured to the full.

'We visited my grandfather and aunties in Stepney very

often and I remember sitting outside the house with grandfather, me on a little stool and him on a fold-up canvas chair (his legs were badly affected by arthritis), and I can see his hands holding the paper. I was perhaps three years old and learning to knit. I can remember his hands, and people going through to the market in Old Road, stopping to talk to him and asking me what I was doing and helping me when I was stuck, the feel of the wool, but not the needles, and then my mother coming out to me and seeing my progress.'

'I remember being cuddled especially when I was ill – my mother tucking me into a nice soft warm bed – the smell of those clean sheets is with me as I type this. I can remember the lovely feeling of security it gave me watching my mother sewing at her sewing-machine when I was ill in bed. Incidentally, I can also remember only too well, as if it were only yesterday, putting flour on my face and pretending I was ill.'

This mother is almost bound to convey the same love and comfort to her children when they are ill – and how easy it is to understand the floury face! You can almost see the child's mind ticking over and working it all out (without even knowing that she did it, let alone how she did it): 'I feel a bit unloved at the moment. I'd like some of her undivided time and attention. When I ask her to come and play with me she says run along because she's busy. How can I get what I want? What's the one certain way of getting her full loving attention? By being ill!' Dimly echoes of parental voices come back – 'She's a bit flushed' (what's that? No help there); 'She's looking a bit pale' (pail? that doesn't make sense); 'He went as white as a sheet'; 'She's better now, but her face is still very white.' White ... White? White! And off she goes to the flour-bin in the hope that playing ill will do the trick.

I remember doing that at school, using talcum powder instead of flour, and it was only looking back years later that I could see that at the time I didn't know any other way of getting the attention other girls seemed to get by being pretty, vivacious, or so vulnerable that people automatically went out of their way to take care of them. I was fat, efficient and officious, with braces round my teeth, and I didn't know how to make a relationship unless it was by looking after or being looked after. The ones I wanted to be with didn't want to be looked after, so I tried to manipulate them into looking after me – without consciously being aware of the fact.

A county director of education has two memories that stay with him still. He lived in a row of terraced houses on a hill in a small mining village in Derbyshire, and can remember lying tucked up in bed and hearing the miners' steel-tipped boots ringing on the cobbles, first very faint as he strained his ears to catch it, then closer and closer, then marching right under his window, and slowly fading into the distance again. He held on to the very last sound. Sometimes it was in the early morning darkness and sometimes when he had just been put to bed at night, and sometimes they were going down the hill and sometimes coming back up the hill. But always he listened for it, and loved it with a private intensity.

His other memory is of 'snow-cold fingers warmed by mother's fire-warmed apron' – which says it all.

Someone else said 'I can remember on Sundays the whole family came to dinner, all the grandparents and aunts and uncles and everyone. And afterwards everyone would go into the front room and my father used to take me on his lap, and they would talk. And I'd lie in his arms and drift off to sleep, and then the voices would come nearer and I'd wake up – then they'd fade away again. It was marvellous, just the warmth and the happiness, being held, and the voices coming and going and coming again in waves.'

There isn't any getting away from the fact that children need our love and our time, and to feel that they matter as a valued person among people. Possessions can never make up for lack of our togetherness with them, and the real togetherness isn't just being in the same house or room, but those times when we are settled in each other's company and enjoying it to the full.

Family circumstances vary tremendously, and in any case it would make growing up and gradual separation very difficult if parent and child are all in all to each other constantly. But it is important that there are times between getting up and going to bed when they know that they have our undivided love and attention. Children have no sense of clock time and bliss can be experienced in minutes rather than hours if we can only recognise and give ourselves wholly to the occasion and to them.

The child of a single working mother could look back to the days when she was delivered to the day nursery each morning and collected in the evening. She didn't remember anything other than 'When she'd collected me from the nursery and we'd got home she would lift me out of the pram and stand cuddling me while we watched the kettle boil. I can remember that.' And it was enough to stay with her all her life.

Chapter 8

Distress

Since children feel so intensely, the opposite of happiness and bliss is better expressed by the word 'distress' rather than 'unhappiness'. The stronger word also conveys the violence of children's reactions to their so-called 'little troubles'. Even little distresses matter intensely while they last.

When my sister and I were children our mother made most of our clothes, or we inherited them from relations and a Mrs Guy altered them to fit. A visit to her upstairs flat was a delight for me, and a misery for my sister. The one room in which she lived and worked was a clutter of bags, suitcases, ornaments, pictures, chairs that couldn't be sat on because other things had got there first, a treadle machine with a carpet of pins and snippets beneath it and a magnificent tailor's dummy looking like a headless Queen Alexandra. Mrs Guy wasn't much bigger than us, a small grey sparrow of a woman who bobbed up and down twittering through a mouthful of pins, miraculously paving the way for us to emerge after the second visit in all the glory of our inherited plumage.

But for my sister it was quite different – she dreaded the visits with all her fastidious heart. The smell of stale air, cabbage water and musty clothes made her take a deep breath before we went in, which she tried to hold until we came out, and in between she held her hankie to her nose. She hated taking her dress off, and visibly withdrew into herself as poor Mrs G knelt to pin her up and looked at her eye to eye through her thick glasses. And when the altered clothes arrived home they had to be washed or cleaned because she couldn't bear the smell which she assured us clung to them. Yet she wasn't fastidious in other ways. We spent hours making mud pies and icing them with ground chalk paste decorated with sawdust chopped nuts and rose petals; and she could clean out the guinea pigs and rabbits quite happily. It was this one room and its occupant that distressed her to the point of revulsion.

I remembered Mrs Guy when a mother described the revulsion she had felt in the close presence of her grandmother. Using her expressive face and hands to highlight the description, she said 'I can remember one of my grandmothers and how I *hated* being kissed. She was huge and droopy, great drooping cheeks and lips and droopy here ... and here ... everywhere. She used to come towards me and bend down with her arms outstretched, and I would back away while my mother's voice would keep saying "Give Grandma a kiss." I *hated* it, it was horrible, and as she got near I could see the hairs on her face, and she smelled of old lady. And then she'd pull me to her and I'd get lost and suffocated in all that flabby mass and smell. Ugh!'

This was real revulsion. In discussion the group was divided. Some felt that parents shouldn't allow, let alone encourage, a child to kiss and be kissed by anyone who revolted them to this degree. Others felt that a few seconds of misery was something a child should put up with in order to make grandparents and others happy.

Parents must work out their own solution, But if someone has to be upset, should it be our child or our parents or in-laws – where does our loyalty lie? If we back up our child, does Grandma have to be let down completely?

We often overrate children's intellectual ability to understand and remember but underrate their perception, for it is possible to say to a child 'I know you don't like kissing Grandma, but we don't want her to feel unloved and unwelcome – could you do something else for her instead?' The child might suggest picking her some flowers, or doing a painting for her, but is just as likely to say 'No' because that expresses the depth of honest feeling.

If so, there may still be a way of working out a compromise if we offer help to avoid the issue whilst explaining that the courtesy of a grandchild to a grandparent must in all other respects be the same as that of a host or hostess to any other guest.

We may be able to say privately to the relative concerned 'Emma has gone off kissing at the moment and we're not forcing it, but I just thought I would tell you'.

On the other hand this may create such a family scene that you can't face it. So why not say so to your offspring? You may still feel you have to say 'Come and kiss Grandma', but at least there would be an honest understanding between you.

Only you know your child, yourself and the power that your upbringing still has over you. Only you know what you can and can't do or say. Only you know whether or not you can look ahead to the time when you may want to say to your teenager 'Don't ever feel you have to kiss, or touch, or be touched by anyone against your will – follow your instincts.' And if you think you may want to say that, now is the time to think about how far conventional behaviour can be allowed to override intuitive feelings working in the opposite direction. The dilemma is real, and it is yet one more example of the way in which being a parent can add depth to our own understanding and integrity.

A woman in her sixties still remembers an aunt from whom she recoiled. 'She was small and silent, with fuzzy hair, dark glasses, a moustache and a far-away voice. I remember she caught me on the landing one day and began to tell me about "your poor dear uncle" in her halting whisper, and warning prickles of 'This is unhealthy, I must get away" galvanised me into backing towards the stairs and dashing down them – I couldn't bear to be in her presence alone.' She was lucky that no one was there to say 'Auntie's talking to you, dear', for she would have been denied the opportunity to obey her real feelings. The older I become the more I regret that so few people are able to be true to their own honest feelings. The habit of not hurting people can become so strong that the self may be denied at a level of real need, and there isn't any guarantee that those 'spared' fare any better, for it may deny them a chance to grow through a temporary upset themselves.

On the other hand it is difficult to recognise the difference between real need and a passing phase, or an excuse for not doing something for trivial reasons, or not doing it in order to punish the one who asks. We all play games of extraordinary complexity, but children are starting at the beginning, and every child offers us an opportunity to become more childlike (not childish) and less devious ourselves.

Sometimes we cause children distress through innocent ignorance of their needs coupled with an upbringing that denied us the expression and satisfaction of those same needs. You don't always consciously miss what you don't have, or you may recognise it and deliberately go to the other extreme. One couple said 'We both came from homes where everything had to be spotless and tidy to the point where cushions were plumped up every time you got out of a chair. Life was one long "Don't do this, don't do that", and we're determined not to inflict that on our children – our home's an absolute tip.' When their children grow up one may want a home to be just the same because it suited him or her to perfection, while the other may recall the muddle with a shudder and create a home where everything is ordered and calm.

Perhaps the area of conflict that most needs to be understood arises when children come to associate the words 'messy' and 'dirty' with 'naughty'. 'Naughty' is something children don't want to be because it cuts them off from the source of love and approval that matters to them so much, but what are they to do when parental 'good' is in direct opposition to their natural 'good'? They become a small but intense battleground of urges: if they obey the urge to please parents and keep clean they have to deny a much stronger natural urge to indulge in messy play with water, sand, mud, clay, paint, dough and paste or glue. According to their temperament they may become reluctant to do anything in case it is 'naughty', or they may whine 'I've got nothing to do' or blow their tops in bursts of aggression.

The stress of being curbed from doing what comes naturally can be heightened if the child goes to a playgroup or nursery school or class where all the other children are playing freely and happily with such forbidden pleasures – or if inexperienced staff or helpers try, for the child's own good, to encourage participation in the tempting activities too quickly.

Imagine it from the child's point of view. The last parental words on leaving were probably 'Goodbye, be a good girl/boy – and don't get dirty.' The child will play with dolls, trains, puzzles, lego and books with great pleasure and satisfaction, for they are new and attractive. The adults are kind and loving, and there is the comforting feeling of 'goodness' whilst playing the morning away.

Eventually the newness wears off and a period of fascinated watching of the messy play takes place, until someone says 'Would you like to do finger painting? Here's an overall. Let's turn up your sleeves. There, now off you go!'

I have watched such children stiffen and put their hands behind them, and the helper may say 'Look, like this. It's all right, come along', and with renewed adult permission the child pokes one cautious finger into the shining paint. The slippery feel is lovely, and the other fingers follow, then the other hand – and then all the fingers and thumbs of both hands are off and away, making trails, crossing them, making swirls and loops, and wiping them all out with the flat of the hand only to start again. The rhythmic working of the fingers, thumbs and wrists begins to establish the skills that will be needed for writing later on, while another need is also being met – that of letting go, for people who grow up unable to let go miss so many pleasures. But the playing child knows none of this: boldness replaces inhibition and as the beautiful 'feel' of it all takes over caution is thrown to the winds. With ever larger movements the child reaches out to make patterns over every available bit of space on the paper or table top – and white cuffs protrude from the overall to become paint-smeared. Then anxiety takes over as the absent mother suddenly becomes stronger than the present helper who is saying things like 'It's all right, Mummy can wash it.' Mummy can indeed, she washes everything in sight and irons it beautifully – but the helper doesn't seem to understand that a naughtiness has been committed or that waiting to be collected is now clouded by anxiety.

One playgroup leader who did this in her early days said 'I always made a point of holding the child's hand and greeting the mother with 'She's had a lovely time finger painting – she wore an overall but I'm afraid her cuffs have got a bit painty. Don't worry, it will wash out.'

She never knew the distress some mothers felt, or how strained the relationship was going home, or the recriminations when the dirty dress was removed and washed, or the admonishments that went on during the journey to the playgroup on the next occasion – until one morning she made her little speech to a mother who said 'That's all right' and smiled. 'Then I suddenly saw something,' the playgroup leader told me. 'She was smiling because she knew that she ought not to mind, but she was only smiling with her mouth – not her eyes. She still minded dreadfully.'

Of course she did! Her whole upbringing, and her way of life that was also part of her attraction for her husband, had come under subtle attack as different standards and values were held up to her. Similar parents who have been made to feel welcome just as they are and involved with their playing children discover for themselves just why children love this form of play so much and will often say '*Now* I know why she loves it. It feels beautiful, doesn't it? And it doesn't make all that much mess if you know how to prepare for it.' No parent deliberately denies a child something that is part of the *natural* process of getting on. Yet to go against one's upbringing requires the basic self-confidence to say to oneself 'I'm not as horrified as I was at first – in fact I think I'll give it a try.' But it takes time for parents to alter the habits of a lifetime and no one must pressure them: the moment of readiness to try must come from within.

On the other hand, a few children and adults don't enjoy having messy hands for reasons that seem to be physical rather than emotional. I have never enjoyed clay much although I took pottery classes for some time, but I love the feel of silky soft dough which is so quick to take up the warmth of one's hands. What matters is that we are all given new opportunities, not just once but again and again, for what was disliked initially may be enjoyed at a later stage.

Children have fears and anxieties according to age, stage and experience. Fear of being lost is a very natural one, and often they will play hiding and finding games not only for the fun and magic of 'Here it is, now it's gone!' but also as though to reassure themselves that what is lost *can* be found.

I have watched disturbed children hiding little cars under sand, or pushing buttons into dough, with fierce tense faces. Often they will add the pressure of both hands to the mass for a few seconds, then off they come and a quick scrabble reveals the hidden object to triumphant cries of 'There it was all the time!' This is the equivalent of saying 'There are times when everyone and everything is on top of me and I feel lost – but it's all right, the bit that is *me* is still there and I've found it again.'

But for goodness' sake don't start to worry every time your child plays hiding-up games! Play fulfils many needs in its own way and the child goes along with it as long as a need of one sort or another is there. As a ninety-year-old who greatly enjoyed observing people used to say, 'I just note, dear, but I say naught.' If we do the same our children can teach us so much.

Sometimes children bring about their own distress by doing something they know to be wrong at the time. Or they do it without thinking, only to realise the minute it is done it shouldn't have been. A mother tells of the time workmen came in to lay an area of concrete outside the back door. 'I remember walking over the wet concrete when the men were having their lunch, getting my shoes covered in it and wiping them with the floor-cloth that Mum always hung over the fence. She blamed the men for ruining it and I never let on – it worried me for ages!'

Surely we can all remember that particular dilemma, wanting to own up to ease our conscience but fearing to do so because at the time the misdemeanour seemed so great that we didn't see how we could be forgiven? Or wanting to own up but knowing that we would rather suffer the burden than face the anger, compared with which the punishment was as nothing.

Balancing the need to confess against the fear of losing love goes on for years and repeats itself in different relationships. We cheat at school because we want to earn the praise of a particular teacher, then, when we receive the teacher's praise, it means nothing because we haven't earned it. We pretend we have read a book because we fear

our colleagues will look down on us if we haven't. We say
'It's all right, it doesn't matter' when it does but we fear the
row that might end the relationship. So often we long to be
honest but lack the courage to face what we imagine the
consequences would be.

Only when we recognise all this in ourselves can we
begin to understand how difficult we sometimes make it for
children when we stand over them in all our size and power
saying 'If you own up I shan't be cross.' Better to offer them
a chance to put things right without a fuss – 'Someone's cut
the end off the toothpaste tube and it's oozing out. One of
you go and put a saucer under it so that it doesn't get
wasted.'

Sometimes our good and generous impulses are seen by
our children in quite a different light, and we are shocked
by their reaction.

'I can remember my fifth birthday. My mother made me a
beautiful dress. Just as we were all ready for the tea party
my thirteen-year-old sister appeared wearing an identical
dress Mum had made for her. It was all too much. I
annointed my sister's hair and dress with the complete
contents of a bottle of syrup of figs. Funny, but I can only
remember the pleasure, not the punishment.'

Devastated as the poor mother must have been, I can
understand how the immediate playing of tit for tat helped
to cancel out feelings that were too intense to be bottled up.
Better that reaction, I think, than the silent submission that
later grumbles on as a grudge. As a result of one such
incident my own sister was wont to say for what seemed
like years 'It's my turn, Brenda had the sugar bun.'

A similar example, with more damaging repercussions
because the relationship between mother and child was
already an unhappy one, was given by a social services
adviser. 'My mother was cold and hard. I had one very
precious toy that I remember vividly: it was a cardboard box
with shapes cut out of the cardboard lining into which
doll's house furniture was slotted and held in place by
elastic bands. I used to take it out and play with it secretly,
and then slot everything back into place again and put it
away. One day it wasn't there. I rushed to Mother and she
said "I gave it away, you never play with it." I could never

put into words what I felt – I rushed to the piano and grabbed the trailing leaves of a beautiful plant and pulled it to the floor and broke it into pieces, and I was glad. Glad I'd spoilt it, glad of the mess, glad she was so angry – which was silly really because I loved that plant.'

It was not silly at all, it was a pure reflex action rather like that of a tennis player who faces a volley smashed across the net at close range, and finds his racket has returned it as of its own accord. How much easier it must have been to accept her mother's anger than the hurt of what she had done to that secretly cherished possession.

The sequel was revealed a few minutes later when she said 'I've just this minute seen that I'm still punishing her. My mother and father live with me now and I keep reminding her of all the terrible things she did. I say "Do you remember such-and-such?" and she says, "Well, what of it? Don't make such a silly fuss." And the more she says it the more I punish her. But perhaps now that I've seen what I'm doing I needn't go on doing it.'

One other distress story stays with me. An education adviser told me: 'I have no memory before I was six. And then one day stands out with crystal clarity. I was the eldest of six children living alone with our mother and she just couldn't cope, and on that day a car came to take us all into care. We got into it and my mother stood in the garden combing her long dark hair. We were being taken away from her, and she cared so little that she just stood combing her hair.'

How could a six-year-old understand that some moments in our lives are so horrific that we can only cling to something small and familiar in an attempt to blot out that which can't be borne? Like the young girl clambering out of the wreckage of a train, with twisted metal, broken glass and the dead and injured lying about her, who just kept saying 'I shall be late for work . . . I shall be late for work.'

But how did it happen that those taking the children into care didn't understand what the mother was going through, and try to explain to the children – all of them, not just the six-year-old – that far from not caring their mother cared very much indeed?

It is so much easier to judge than to understand, for to

judge is only to see how others differ from ourselves and say 'Why don't they do what I do? How mistaken and inadequate they are.' To understand means seeing ourselves and all our weaknesses in others. We don't even need to forgive them, because we know exactly how it came about.

So it is with children. Certainly there are things they do that we can't allow, but if we can at least remember doing them ourselves we may be able to remember which were the adults who understood – and what *they* said and did in those circumstances.

There need to be times when we stand back and watch our children, just as an ornithologist watches a bird focused sharply in his binoculars and strives to take in every detail before it flies off again. Only then do we begin to understand the significance of what we see, and act more easily in accordance with what we understand.

Chapter 9

Pattern

As I listened to these random early memories I gradually registered that an awareness of, and feeling for, pattern was emerging in ways that were new to me.

I was familiar with the early stages of young children's paintings, particularly the beautiful stage of spontaneous pattern-making when a child will use three or four brushes from pots of different colours and apply patches of paint to the paper with considered care. Sometimes the patches will be laid close beside each other, and sometimes islands of paint in one colour will be carefully placed before a second colour is used to make other islands, and then the intervening spaces are filled in to give an overall mass of colours, touching but not mixing, balanced into a harmonious whole. This exercise is quite unlike the early random painting when the joy is in covering the paper with paint, or in using different colours just for fun and interest – a by-product of which may be the accidental mixing of two colours to create an unexpected third colour, whereupon another stage of painting is discovered.

But pattern-making is something different: it is careful and considered, and is continued until it comes to what the child recognises as the end – often a final standing back to contemplate the apparently finished work of art will result in a brushful of paint being used to add one or more last spots of paint deliberately placed. Or the pattern may be more formal, taking the form of strong stripes of colour, usually vertical but sometimes in rainbow formation, or a series of spaces contained by a line and filled with spots, crosses, dashes or textured in some other way.

A final inspection marks the end of a totally absorbing episode, and the child often has no further need of the end product.

In many playgroups and nurseries children's paintings are named and taken home to give parents pleasure, and it therefore becomes important to the children that they don't go home without them. But if this custom has not been established it is rare for a child to want to keep a painting or to give it to someone.

Where no end product is expected or given undue importance and children can paint as freely as they handle clay, dough or sand the activity is an end in itself. The period of painting is one of dreamy concentration and satisfaction, followed by release when the child emerges from the oblivion of his or her own world and rejoins the human race, calm and satisfied.

Picture-making comes later, but still the feeling for pattern is there. It may be strong or delicate in colour and brushwork, but it flows and expands with a feeling of freedom and balance.

The painting of disturbed children often lacks this feeling of balance and pattern. Sometimes cramped little brush-strokes are confined to one small corner of the paper, or maybe there is the endless repetition of a dot surrounded by concentric circles. Perhaps the latter is a symbol of the 'me' that is hemmed in by anxiety, fear or lack of self-esteem, then as confidence grows the repeated pattern often becomes larger and bolder until the day arrives when it is slashed by lines like the radiation of the sun and the child is freed to break out and paint prolifically. Or one day it may just be forgotten and a new form of painting will take its place, to coincide with a marked step forward in the child's general confidence and happiness.

It is important not to read too much into children's paintings, especially as those starting for the first time at five or six will go through all the stages that early painters discover at eighteen months or two years. They are not backward, just beginning later. Similarly, many children will try out what they have seen others do, or may lose their freedom of style temporarily if they have a setback in other directions, which serves to emphasise that in painting a child can often express what can't at that particular moment be expressed in any better way.

Painting play can soothe and unravel, give vent to bottled up feelings or be an outward expression of an inner creativity as children work their way towards a state of harmony in which they are free to 'flow' – as long as the process is allowed to run its natural course in its own time. If they are interrupted the spell is almost always broken and they are left stranded halfway between where they were in their own private world and where they are back in our world. The result is usually an end to the painting without the fulfilment which characterises a child who has 'finished'.

Gradually, I became aware that certain memories were adding a new dimension to what I already knew about the pattern of children's painting, and the pattern of their patterns.

Some of you may recognise in the following memories a psychological significance that I have missed; and some of the examples I have chosen may well have arisen from a source quite different from the one to which I have attributed them. But I don't think any of this matters much if only we can become more aware of what children do, and their feelings as they do it. If we can catch a memory flash of having done the same thing we may have the sudden understanding to leave them alone, or to break in if we have to with a fellow feeling for their point of view as well as our own.

The memory which first made me sit up and take notice came from a mother who vividly recalled an episode in Sainsbury's when she was about two and a half years old. She remembered the shop from many such visits, with the tiled walls and their inlaid murals of a giant bull, pig, cow and sheep. The marble-topped counters ran down each side and it was necessary to queue separately for the butter, cheese, sausages and dry goods – which made shopping a long and boring business for a child.

But on this occasion it was far from boring. Sitting on the floor, she became aware of the blue and white mosaic tiles patterned in scrolls and squiggles. The tiles were smooth and cool and she was following the blue pattern with her finger, hitching along when the next bit of the squiggle was out of reach. Suddenly her mother, realising where she was and what she was doing, picked her up and dumped her unceremoniously on the pram seat. Screaming, kicking, she tried to get down, and there was a split second when she 'knew' that her mother thought she was throwing a tantrum – but she was powerless to explain that she just *had* to finish tracing out the pattern and how exciting it was. She can still recapture that feeling of fury and indignation, and powerlessness to explain.

The mother probably feared that her child would be trodden on, so no wonder she dived quickly to retrieve her and put her in the safety of the pram without losing her place in the queue. But if she had understood the child's compulsion to complete the pattern it might have been possible to break into her concentration more gently, and the child might have come out of her private world more easily and consented to being put back into the pram without the added wear and tear on both of them of the screaming.

An Irish journalist remembers kneeling under larch trees and raking the dry dust and fallen larch needles into runnels with wide-spaced fingers, then building up the ridges into parallel lines that were higher and deeper than before. Then came the gathering of larch cones and the careful grading of them by size, the smaller ones being set up on top of the front ridge, the medium ones on the second ridge, and the largest ones on the back ridge. 'I can remember the depth of concentration, and how terribly important it was that every cone was exactly the right size, and that they were placed exactly the same distance apart. It was immensely satisfying kneeling there in the sun, working so meticulously.'

If children have this deep desire to follow a course of feeling-inspired action to their perceived ending, I find myself wondering how often we interrupt them abruptly or unnecessarily in mid-task. Sometimes it has to be done – a whole row of tulip heads snapped off is a sacrifice most parents won't feel called upon to make – but if we could learn to recognise and allow natural periods of concentrated effort to run their course perhaps later on fewer school reports would comment 'Lacks concentration'.

In the exhausting early years of parenthood, weariness and habit lead us to say 'Don't touch', 'Don't do that', 'Come here' and 'What are you doing?' almost as a reflex action whenever our children are suspiciously quiet or we haven't given ourselves time to see what they are actually doing. Inevitably we look at their busy hands first, but if we could also look at the concentration on their faces we might perhaps leave them alone more often than we do, to await the moment when a 'proper' ending affords them the satisfaction that each of us knows so well in our own lives as we bring something to a conclusion.

Another interesting memory referred to the power that a particular pattern held over a grandmother in her youth. Her daughter said 'My mother was at her sewing-machine one day recently when she suddenly called out *"There* it is! The pattern . . . that's the pattern."* I went to her and she showed me the squiggly pattern on her old Singer sewing-machine – a sort of intertwined emblem on the black bit above the needle. She was laughing and excited and nearly crying. She said when she was a little girl she used to have terrible dreams of dragons chasing her, and she'd wake up and never could explain what had frightened her. And now, machining busily as she had done for years, she had suddenly "seen" the pattern and recognised it in a sort of flash. She got down on the floor and looked up at it, which was the view she would have had as a child sitting by her mother as the sheets were sides-to-middled and the curtains made – and there was the "monster" twirling on the black background exactly as she remembered it.'

I pondered the question of pattern: children's patterns on paper; our own pattern-making as we move furniture around to create the most pleasing room possible; children placing cones, shells and buttons with ordered precision; our bedding-out of plants in rows, curves or clumps – I am sure I am not the only one who has replanted a seedling that was out of position, even though it would scarcely be noticed when they were all in bloom. There *is* something compelling about pattern for its own sake.

Children follow a squiggly pattern with a finger, we follow a train of thought through loops and whorls as we try to get to the point of resolve. Is one stage the forerunner of the other? If we are spoken to at the crucial moment just before that elusive something is within our conscious grasp we say 'Hold it, just a minute. No, it's no good – it's gone.

Perhaps it will come back.' But the chances are it doesn't, and we feel let down and cut off. No wonder the child in Sainsbury's screamed with frustration!

The real pattern on the sewing-maching was transposed into a nightmare. I know a type of dream that I recognise as having a special quality even as I dream it; then comes the sensation of rising to the surface through deep water. Just before I break surface there is a flash of 'knowing' and I have to hold back long enough for the fantasy to be transposed into reality. I wake with a problem resolved, or a new insight as to how to proceed with something, or with comprehension illuminating what has previously been mystifying. And with this quality of 'knowing' there is no doubting, it has its own unmistakable certainty.

There is a thread running through all this which at the back of my mind is linked to a September morning on the farm when I was fourteen. I woke up knowing that the light was strange and not grasping what it was – it was a devastating early frost and the window-panes were thickly encrusted with frost in beautiful feathery fronds. I opened the window and the early sun sparkled on rime-encrusted leaves and grass, and the pampas grasses by the gate looked like plumes of spun sugar. It was breathtakingly beautiful, but cold enough for me to beat a hasty retreat to the icy bathroom, then down to breakfast. Mother was near to tears. The dahlia border which she had worked for since she had lifted and stored the tubers ten months ago was a black petrified forest. The evening before it had been full of the promise of eight weeks of glorious flowers of every size, colour and shape, each chosen with particular rooms, alcoves, wall-brackets and vases in mind.

Not one had survived. And as the sun warmed and thawed the ice crystals, so the blackened heads and leaves drooped sodden and slimy.

No sooner had I adjusted my mood to hers than my father came in from the farm – on top of the world. The harvest stubble had recently been ploughed in and the frost had broken up the ground perfectly in preparation for harrowing.

I sat between them suddenly understanding that there is a pattern and harmony in the natural course of events which is nevertheless devastating to individual interests. It was a revelation that has stayed with me.

Many children seem so at home in a beautiful state of being and knowing, living in harmony with life – but that harmony includes violent ups and downs, it is not the smooth level of niceness that we somehow expect and see as desirable. Perhaps children are wiser than we are – they accept our lapses from 'goodness' more forgivingly than we accept theirs. They accept and respond to the rhythm of activity and rest, talking and silence, anger and calm, anguish and peace, aloneness and togetherness – or they could if only we would accept all their moods and learn to respond to them appropriately.

Think of the child arranging larch cones, with solitude and all the time in the world in which to expand. But what if we had walked that way? Would we have understood the perfection of that timeless play and withdrawn quietly? Or would we have called out cheerfully 'There you are! I wondered where you were, it's time for dinner' or 'Hello, what are you doing? What a lot! One, two, three, four' or 'How lovely . . . all in rows . . . could you make a square?' or 'Larch cones! We've got a book about coniferous trees indoors, shall we go and find it?' or 'Look at you, you're covered in those wretched little needles, they'll block up the washing-machine'? Still I ponder. In the early years of founding a family there are so many practicalities to attend to, so much discussion centred on day-to-day decisions, so much guilt associated with wasting time, so much pressure felt to get on and get the children on, so much will-power expended to keep going. When I was young I tried hard to live positively and work for what I wanted (or thought I ought to want), and to be strong enough to overcome obstacles. Two hard blows in quick succession taught me that it was a source of much greater strength to accept my vulnerability and just get on with what I had to do. I also learned to follow rather than lead – a concept of living that I would have considered feeble in my youth (which it probably would have been at that stage). Now I find that one event, or person, leads to another, that things often happen through rather than by me. There are intricate chains of events of which I am part.

Chapter 10

'Now they'll never know . . .!'

After pondering somewhat philosophically and inconclusively the significance of pattern in children's play and the part pattern plays visibly and invisibly throughout our lives, it was refreshing to be confronted with a memory unlike any I had met before.

I had been talking at a county family day and at the end asked if anyone had been reminded of an early episode in their own lives. A grandmother said 'Yes! It took me right back . . . I was about three, I suppose. I was standing by the kitchen table looking at a bowl of tomatoes and wanting one. I looked at them for a long time, then I gave in and took one and took a bite out of it. Then I panicked and I couldn't take another mouthful. Then I had a wonderful idea and knew exactly what I had to do. I put it back and took a bite out of another one – then put that back and took a bite out of the next one. I knew if I had only had time to take a bite out of each they would all be the same and no one would ever know!'

There was a gale of laughter, then something suddenly flashed into my own mind. I was sitting on the edge of my bench in a maths lesson – truly trying to understand, and knowing that the moment was fast approaching when I would have to give up inside myself but would smile and nod and say 'Yes, thank you' when the master had explained it yet again and said 'All right now?' What he was trying to explain was that if you did the same thing to both sides of an equation you didn't alter anything, it was still the same, but I didn't see how you could alter something without altering it.

Gran had been better than both of us – she had just 'known' it!

I went to another county playgroup day and told them

about Gran among other memories. Afterwards the principal of the local teacher training college, who had chaired the meeting, said 'I was gripped by Gran for she suddenly explained something which happened at home when we were children. My father had planted some little apple trees at the end of the lawn and we had them for a year or two before they were allowed to bear fruit. On this particular year each branch that carried apples was allowed to bear just one, and its weight bent the branch down so that all the fruit was quite near the ground. One morning we went out and found that someone had taken a bite out of an apple without removing it from the tree – then we discovered a tiny bite had been taken out of every other apple, not only on that tree but on all the others. Nothing was ever said about it, but I remember we were all fairly sure that it was the youngest in the family!'

I met the same memory a third time, and this one many people must have experienced for themselves. The link adviser between a college of further education and the local primary schools and playgroups recalled sitting on the stairs and pressing her finger on one of the raised petals of the flowered Lincrusta wallpaper. 'I squashed it flat and it felt most satisfying, so I squashed the one next to it, then the next, and the next. I couldn't stop but I began to feel anxious and it was a relief when I had completed the whole flower. But then I saw how different that flower looked to the one on the next step and I knew I'd have to do the same to that one too. I went from step to step trying to do them all before I was caught – but I was caught, of course, and got into terrible trouble.'

Other remember using a pencil or crayon in the same way – filling in patterns at first by happy accident, then being compelled to complete the pattern for its own sake, then being driven by anxiety to 'do the same to all of them so no one will ever know'.

As this is so common it seems sensible to try to avoid the wallpaper temptation at least – which many parents do by using washable emulsion paint or vinyl wallpaper, or using the paper of their choice in one room which they guard quite carefully, or by allowing their children to choose a paper for their bedroom that will be their pride and joy. But this doesn't mean that the joy of 'popping' raised paper patterns, or colouring them, has to be forfeited. Books of obsolete wallpaper patterns are a great joy for which children find endless use in one way or another. I know one home day nursery where the husband and wife have used these books to make a delightful patchwork round the lower three feet of the play-room walls. If one patch is defaced it can be removed and replaced, and the children are free to wander, look, touch and enjoy in a very positive way. There is very little damage done, and where it is they accept it as one of the hazards of having children and replace the patch without fuss.

If you can't find an old pattern book odd rolls of wallpaper can be bought quite cheaply in sales, cut into large pieces and attached with clothes-pegs to a piece of soft board which can be laid flat on the floor (better than a table because more pressure can be brought to bear), propped against the wall, or stood on the seat of a hard chair leaning against the back like an easel. The firmness of the backing and the smooth immobility of the paper are important, otherwise the satisfaction is decreased to the point where interest is lost.

It can't be said too often, children *must* play, and there has to be somewhere where they can be free to learn by trial and error without parents being upset. Yes, they do have to learn to respect property, but if the property is always held to be more important than their play the lessons they learn may be inhibition and guilt without the benefits of real play.

A compromise is needed: either have children before the house is got right; or, if it is just as you like it before children arrive, then prepare as you would for a puppy and remove everything that could be damaged by small teeth, grubby paws and a tendency to knock things over.

If children were houseplants they would arrive with a small 'how to care for' leaflet saying 'Regular feeding, warm temperature, allow plenty of room for sprawling growth'. And we would obey the instructions – or else not buy the plant at all.

A grandfather recalled something he'd done when he was about four years old: 'It was the First World War and we were staying in a boarding-house. In the dining-room there was a long shelf and each guest had his own tin of condensed milk. Well, I slipped in there one day and I just couldn't resist putting my finger in one of the tins and having a lick. I shouldn't have done it but I couldn't help myself – and once I'd started I couldn't stop! But I had a brainwave. I thought if I take just one lick out of each of them they'll all be the same and it won't matter. So I did. But I got caught, and were they angry!'

Back into my mind flashed the sequel to Gran and her tomatoes. She had managed to take a bite from each before her mother found her, and it must have been bitterly disappointing to discover that her confident plan hadn't worked – because her mother did notice what she had done, and was very cross indeed. 'She said "What did you do that for?" But I had my answer ready. "Because they made me!" I told her.'

Both Gran and Grandad spoke the truth when they said of the tomatoes and the condensed milk 'They made me' and 'I couldn't stop'. We have to eat to live, and nature has planned for everything to work together to that end: there is a mechanism that tells us when we are hungry, and as an extra inducement to eat there is the sight and smell of food. Further, if the sight and smell arouse memories of previous enjoyment of those foods the salivary glands begin to secrete their juices and our mouths literally water.

Those children were exposed full-force to one of the most natural pleasures in the world, to which they would have responded naturally by eating as much as they wanted until they were full – if it hadn't been for one thing. They were beginning to learn from their parents about right and wrong: not the spontaneous right and wrong of nature, but the restrictions which have to modify natural instincts if life is to be civilised and manageable.

They both knew that what they wanted to do was 'wrong'. But Gran didn't know that a tomato with a hole in it would shrivel round the edges and not keep, or that other members of the family might find it unattractive to be offered a nibbled tomato. And Grandad didn't understand the tight restriction of rationing whereby some people might be done out of one extra cup of tea, nor did he know about germs from dirty fingers, or the spread of germs from one tin to another. Neither of them really understood the personal nature of property (the difficulty here is that so often personal toys are offered to the baby to play with without their owner's consent, or a precious stick or stone is thrown away as 'rubbish'). What both of them *did* know was that grown-ups, particularly parents, would be cross.

There they were, face to face, nose to smell, with food. Nature said 'Come on', and the memory of past and future anger said 'You mustn't.' The food won, as it was bound to do at that age and stage – unless the real fear of parents was so cripplingly strong that it had already crushed natural instinct. And who would want to do that? Certainly no one who has cause to wish that some of his or her natural instincts hadn't been so inhibited in childhood that the repercussions carried on into adult life.

In addition to the magnetic pull of food I wonder whether there was the additional pull of the desire to complete a task? The Grandfather said 'Once I'd started I couldn't stop', and I have a feeling that even if he had begun to feel a bit sick by the nineteenth lick he might still have felt compelled to reach the twenty-fourth tin.

We know so little about children and expect so much from them. They have to learn to accept family rules, but I think they could learn more effectively if we reacted consistently but more gently with these early misdemeanours. Many of the thirteen- and fourteen-year-old schoolboys who wrote about their fears came out strongly with the observation that 'being shouted at' was still what they dreaded most.

Later I learned more about the drive to make things equal, though not always with the feeling that if they are the same no one will know.

A young mother told us this tale about her three-year-old daughter. 'I had been saving for ages to buy some Laura Ashley material to make new curtains for the sitting-room, and at last I had enough and Emma and I went to buy it together. I cut them out and made them in stages. I got as far as making them, hanging them to check the hem and pinning them up, and spread them out on the floor to tack before machining them. They were there for several days, and one day Emma came to me beaming just as I was dishing up the dinner and said "Come and see what I've done!" She took me by the hand and led me to the sitting-room – she had made two identical oblique cuts right across both curtains, having "made" them for me. But it was as you said: the cuts and holes in each curtain matched exactly.'

We all asked with bated breath what she had done, and with a sweetness that matched Emma's she said 'I couldn't be cross, she was looking at me with such delight, so sure she had "helped" – and the curtains were ruined anyway. I cut them smaller for Emma's room and she's *delighted* with the curtains "she made", and *loves* the holes she made, and takes everyone upstairs to show them.'

Although the sitting-room continued to have shrunk and faded curtains I feel sure this family gained far more than it lost through the generosity of heart of Emma's mother.

Another mother in this same group said 'That reminds me of another story concerning curtains. My neighbour's little girl, she's six, had been very naughty one day so her mother told her to go upstairs and stay in her bedroom. When she went up to her later she found that she had got hold of a pair of scissors and made a six-inch cut just above the hem of the curtain – only she hadn't just done it once, she'd done it both sides of both curtains. And later my friend discovered that she had done it to every curtain in all the bedrooms. Do you think she suddenly realised what she'd done and tried to hide it by doing it to all the other curtains?'

I don't know, but I should be surprised if it was merely coincidence because evidence seems to be stacking up to suggest that children just might have a natural feeling for mathematical laws. I shall continue to listen and learn with great interest but, if anyone says to me 'Ah! pre-maths experience', I shall feel tempted to reply 'You have already killed the butterfly by pinning it down with your jargon.'

Chapter 11

'Good' or 'Naughty'?

A friend had come to tea and I helped to set the table and prepare the food, but at the last minute I had a brainwave and thought watercress with the sardine sandwiches would be a good idea. I dashed into the pantry, found the bundle that was planned for a later meal, ripped off the rubber band, plonked the watercress in a dish and put it on the table just as everybody sat down.

Mother looked at the assorted stalks and roots and just said in a quiet aside 'Did you wash the watercress?' I knew at once that I'd missed out both the washing and the picking over, and grabbed the dish to rectify matters. As I disappeared Mother called out 'Wash it well, darling', and determined to excel this time I filled the bowl with water, tipped the watercress in, and then picked up a handful at a time and rubbed it well with carbolic soap.

I don't remember what was said or done after my return – I just remember eating a mouthful and being thunderstruck that the watercress tasted like the carbolic soap smelled.

A mother remembered getting into terrible trouble as a young child because she had torn a whole handful of pages out of a book. She said 'The storm broke so suddenly, and I was so shocked, that I couldn't explain – I just burst into tears. And I never did explain because I was so hurt. I remember exactly what I had done, and why. It was a story-book with quite a lot of plain written pages and only a few pictures. There was the picture of a girl on one page, playing by herself. And several pages further on there was a boy, and he was alone, too. So I thought if I took the middle pages out they would be able to play with each other when the book was shut.'

No wonder it hurt to be accused of spoiling the book when she had acted with such loving kindness to the children *in* the book and had worked out their problem so intelligently. This mother was also a teacher and she said how very careful the memory had made her in mediating between children and books, and we all agreed with her view that we musn't become too precious about books. It isn't any good preaching that children must have 'good books', and be read to if we don't understand the impact the stories between the covers will have on some children.

I can remember going through a childhood book of my mother's. It had fawn woolly-surfaced pages and a green cover with 'Stories To Tell The Littlest Ones' lettered in gold. I knew it by heart, but on this occasion I sat down with great purpose and two pieces of blackboard chalk, pale blue and brown, with which to carry out my plan. I went through the book very slowly and carefully and all the nasty characters were blocked out with the brown chalk, and my favourite ones – especially the little bull calf – were covered in beautiful pale blue as a token of love.

We must be clear about our priorities: we can't have our book and tear it. The importance of a book lies in what it can do to and for each particular child who looks at it, or to whom it is read. There is a relationship between a child and a book, varying from mild interest to fascination, from strong liking to disliking or a love-hate, love-fear relationship. There is an emotional response to colour, to the pictures themselves, to the characters and to the unfolding of the story. There is the delight of mastery, of knowing what comes next, of knowing it by heart and pretending to 'read' it. In any relationship there is a response, and occasionally the response leads to the book being defaced in one way or another. At that point we have to decide which matters most, the book itself or the motives which prompted the child to act. If the damage is already done when we come upon the scene, then the most helpful thing is to try to discover what's going on without a probing or an accusing approach. If the child had been able to explain about the children playing together the mother could have said 'What a good idea. And if we tape the pages together they can go in the back of the book ready for when we want to read the story next time.' The repair of damage teaches care of books even more effectively than the prohibition of damage, or punishment.

I remember in the early 1970s a high-powered meeting

at which a publisher called together a group of people from the playgroup movement, nursery schools, training colleges and universities to advise them on how to proceed in the under-five market that had just been discovered.

At one point everyone seemed to be agreeing that books in which animals dressed and behaved as human beings were to be avoided at all costs. I said many children loved and needed them. There was a strained silence, broken by a university lecturer saying 'Well, of course, if you're the sort of woman who *likes* stories about mice dressed up in knickers, there's no more to be said.'

But there was, and is. As children struggle to learn about goodness and badness, obedience and disobedience, rewards and punishments, kindness and unkindness, they are dealing with very powerful feelings within themselves – but sometimes they can't take it unless it comes to them at one remove. A rabbit can behave badly, a hen can be nearly caught by a wicked fox, a kitten can be lost on a cold dark night, and the tension is only bearable for some children if the victim or culprit feels and behaves like a child but isn't one.

On the other hand some children enjoy tales about other naughty children, or children who run into danger of one kind or another. Stories matter in these early years for they speak to children in specific ways. In addition to giving great pleasure, and providing togetherness with us, they help children to become familiar with the various ways in which adults use words like 'good' and 'bad' and 'naughty' – and it certainly takes a bit of sorting out when we see ourselves as children see us!

The mother of a three-year-old told how she had opened the front door to find the paper and three bottles of milk on the step, and said 'Drat! I only wanted two.' She picked up the paper and two of the bottles to carry them through to the kitchen. As she returned for the third bottle she heard the crash of broken glass and saw her daughter leaning over the gate looking at the broken milk bottle she had just thrown on to the pavement. 'What on earth are you doing?' she called out angrily, and as the child turned she saw her face change from innocent satisfaction to shock and tears.

Anger, defiance and distress mingled as the child cried 'But you said you didn't want the other one.'

Another child picked a bunch of flowers for her mother and when she was asked where they came from said quite happily 'Next door.' The mother was horrified, but she needn't have been. Yes, technically speaking it was stealing, but her son wasn't a thief – he was just a little boy who hadn't yet grasped property laws, boundaries, privacy and all the adult complications of bad feeling between neighbours. He just saw some lovely flowers, wanted to give them to his mother, and walked through the open gate to pick them for her with no attempt at concealment – he didn't even know there was anything to conceal.

I remember doing exactly the same thing and mother explaining that the flowers in Mrs Long's garden belonged to Mrs Long, so we had better take them back to her. She wasn't cross and although my gift had fallen flat I felt nothing more – until we knocked on Mrs Long's door and were waiting for her to open it. Then I suddenly 'saw' what I had done and was frightened. Mrs Long was splendid. Mother did all the explaining, I was forgiven and we were invited in. I was taken through to the kitchen to watch the finding of a vase and the arranging of the flowers. She put them on the window-sill, said how nice they looked and how pleased she was to have them there. Then we went home.

She could so easily have been cross, or worse still have said 'That's all right, you can have them.' What a terrible reproach they would have been at home!

Another mother wrote: 'I remember being puzzled that my mother wasn't pleased with a bunch of flowers I had picked for her because they had come from the garden of a burned-out house. I was three at the time.'

If only we could 'see' through the eyes of a child we would see innocence instead of guilt, and our teaching would be gentler and more appropriate.

The most poignant story of all came from Ireland. When I asked if anyone had been reminded of any incident in their own childhood there was silence. Then a lovely girl, shaking with nerves in the face of such a large meeting, stood up supported by a chair-back and

'Yes. When I was about three I thought I would give my mother a surprise and decided to scrub the two steps that went down from the kitchen to the living-room. I got as much water as I could carry in a pail, and I tipped a whole packet of detergent in because I wanted them to be cleaner than they had ever been before. I knew exactly how they should be scrubbed because I had watched Mother do it so many times, and as I scrubbed this way and that, with two hands and with one, I thought how pleased she would be. Suddenly her voice shouted "What ever are you doing?" It made me jump, and I turned quickly – and knocked the pail over. It was terrible. I knelt there with the soapy water pouring over the steps, and swishing sideways up the wall, and going down over the next step. And then I saw the carpet at the bottom – it had turned black. I couldn't move.

'And then Mother was shouting "Go upstairs – up to your room – now this minute", and I shot past her through the kitchen to the stairs. She chased after me, grabbing up a wooden spoon from the kitchen. She hit me once on every step. And my room was up two flights to the attic. I can remember it now. I was sobbing, and the spoon kept hitting me on my calf, and my thigh, and my bottom – wherever she could get me as I dodged from one side to the other. I grabbed the stair rail and tried to climb up quickly, then scrambled on all fours. Sobbing and trying to get out of the way.

'When I got to my room Mother shut me in, and I cried and cried. Not just because it stung where I had been hit but because she hadn't understood that I was giving her a surprise.

'Eventually she came up – I don't know how long it was and she was crying. She gathered me up in her arms and rocked me saying "Forgive me . . . forgive me . . . you were trying to help and I didn't see it. Forgive me." And, do you know, from that minute everything was all right. I didn't mind about my legs or anything – as soon as I knew she understood about the surprise everything was all right.'

We had listened in total silence, with her all the way, flinching with her on every stair. And I felt others in that hall were sharing my thoughts about atonement – the at-one-ment which is total forgiveness.

Just as we were all beginning to breathe again the postscript came. 'The sad thing is that my mother has never been able to forgive herself. She is seventy-four now, and she still talks about it and every time her eyes fill with tears. I've told her and told her that it was all right as soon as she cuddled me and said that she understood, but she can't forgive herself.'

We can all miss the mark with our children in the heat or blindness of the moment, and it is salutary to be reminded that children are able to forgive and forget once things are put right – so why can't we forgive ourselves?

The pattern is there if we can only see and follow where it leads. We are going to make mistakes, so are they, again and again because we are all only human – and if we don't make mistakes we do not learn. So, since we can't avoid making mistakes, we need to have the insight to recognise them when we do.

In theory, at least, all we have to do is suffer the shock waves as we go down in our own esteem, swallow the pride and fear that make us want to be right all the time and in control all the time, and be so much more aware of the distress we have caused than of our own distress that we risk everything to say 'I'm sorry'. And having taken the risk, we almost always find that there is reconciliation.

Why is it so difficult? Many parents have said to me over the years 'I can't say I'm sorry. I don't know why but I just can't bring myself to say the actual words even when I am – not to my children, or my husband.' This is an experience that most of us will recognise. Usually we are able to overcome it, but it clearly helps if we can discuss our own feelings when we're at the crisis point, or soon after.

'I feel I can't afford to be wrong, I've put everything into being a wife and mother and if I'm not good at that there's nothing left for me to be good at.'

This myth needs to be exploded and I feel it can not be said too often that being a parent offers a unique opportunity to undo some of the knots that bind us, to relearn from and with our children, and to discover that the necessary early sacrifice of ourselves for our children need not be a martyrdom but can be creative.

People talk about becoming a cabbage at home. As a farmer's daughter I don't see it like that at all! A much more accurate simile is to see the home as a greenhouse where new plants are germinated slowly – neither stunted nor forced – and the less hardy ones are brought in from the cold to be nurtured so that they may grow and bloom more prolifically when they are set out later. Parenthood can be exactly like this, a preparation for a new and creative stage of life that can be taken up in various ways as the demands of children lessen and change.

'If the children find me out they'll lose their respect for me.'
The very opposite is true. Most of us can remember the time when we thought our parents were infallible – able to answer all questions, mend anything that was broken, and cope with an emergency. But the chances are that when we eventually 'found them out' it was in adolescence and we agreed with our friends that parents were pretty dim – only to discover a few years later still that they had improved greatly. Or we carried on idealising them and copying them without growing up to accept the responsibility of working things out for ourselves instead of living by, and handing on, an unquestioned set of habits and responses.

It is still true that children need us to act in an emergency, to take over and assume complete responsibility until it can be shared. It is still true that parents need to answer questions – but they can't possibly know the answers to all the specific questions, and this doesn't matter in the least because from the child's point of view it is very reassuring to be told 'I don't know, who do you think we could ask?' For my money, asking *people* is more helpful than looking in books in the early years. It helps children to know that nobody has the answer to everything, but everybody has the answer to something. Reliance on the accuracy of books can be misleading. A book can be factually accurate about plants, electricity, geography – but what happens when it comes to politics and economics, and above all child-rearing?

'I'm frightened of losing control'.
The National Childbirth Trust are learning from each other

as much as they can about depression, and one interesting discovery is that one of the common characteristics among those who suffer from depression is their feeling that they *have* to be in control all the time. This was true for me, and of many others with whom I have talked – we have to keep up with everything, not let anything slip, be the perfect answer to everyone's problems, have the house looking good, the meals on time. Not (as I once thought) because we feel we owe it to everyone, or because we flatter ourselves that we can take all this in our stride – but (I now see) because of the unacknowledged fear that if we once let go we would roll down an invisible hill into goodness knows what abyss. Or because we fear that if we don't control people and events they will control us. This isn't to suggest that children need us to 'lose control' of ourselves or them, but they do need us not to *need* to control them: they need us to be relaxed about their mistakes and ours, they need us to help them to put their mistakes right and to see and hear us helping to put our own mistakes right. It has to be a two-way sharing of experience.

I knew a nine-year-old who couldn't bring herself to say 'I'm sorry' until one day out of the blue she discovered the magic word. 'I'm sorry, I've left the door open', 'I'm sorry, I'm eating too quickly', 'I'm sorry, I've got your chair', 'I'm sorry, I haven't cleaned out the guinea pig' – the apologies went on and on, including for many things that weren't, and never had been, 'wrong'. And finally, at the end of the day, she said 'Saying "I'm sorry" is perfectly easy once you get the knack, isn't it?' Try it.

'I'm frightened of losing their love'.
This is the saddest reason of all, for so often it means that throughout childhood, in spite of many proofs of real love, the impression has slowly grown that the 'better' you are the more love you can earn. Love can rarely be earned, and never in this way. If this fits you, take every opportunity to show your children that you love them not only in success but also in failure – more, that you don't think in terms of failure but of mistakes, or helpful signs that enable you all to learn about your present strengths and limitations. In the

words of a card which I came across in a hospital some years ago:

'I do my thing, and you do your thing.
I am not in this world to live up to your expectations
And you are not in this world to live up to mine.
You are you, and I am I,
And if by chance we find each other it's beautiful:
If not, it can't be helped.'

We and our children grow and develop at our own rate, and from time to time we do lose each other – unless we conspire unconsciously to pour them into our mould in the hope that they will set like small jelly baby replicas of us, which heaven forbid!

We have to set broad guidelines, and agree a few of our own family rules, but what we *are* will set them a pattern that they may find quite hard to break. Therefore we need to be careful that our pattern is not too restrictive, but even more careful that we do not fail to offer a consistent pattern at all.

The pattern we acquire in childhood is usually stronger than we realise, and departing from it in later years can give rise to feelings of guilt even when they aren't appropriate – as I discovered when I began to write. By trial and error I learned that I write best from 7.30 a.m. to noon or beyond according to how it is going, and that I write most comfortably in bed with three pillows stuffed behind my back and my knees drawn up to support my clipboard and pad. But I cannot rid myself of feeling guilty at being in bed when I'm not ill!

Barbara Cartland would be pleased with me as I emerge from the bathroom in glamorous writing attire and ensconce myself in the back writing-bedroom. But the phone rings and as I pick up the receiver I can feel myself reaching for a jumper-and-skirt voice as though my guilty secret could somehow waft down the wires. And the doorbell is a thousand times worse. In the early days I was sorely tempted to give a rasping cough as I undid the latch in the hope that the caller would attribute my housecoat to flu. My intelligence tells me I am not guilty of anything,

I am merely suffering from an overdose of childhood conditioning. I was set such a high standard that, without the words actually being spoken at all, I came to believe that anyone who was fit and well and not down to breakfast bright and early, properly washed and dressed, was a slut.

Parents can't win. Whatever we do or don't do our children will look back and be grateful for so much, as well as regretful in other ways. And that is 'right', not 'wrong'.

Chapter 12

Copycat

Grandfather used to say that imitation was the sincerest form of flattery, but I distinctly remember at school that if any of us adopted this form of flattery then our new hairstyle, way of talking, or latest acquisition was greeted with shouts of 'Copycat! Copycat!' This was enough to put some people off trying again, which was a pity because unless we can imitate what we see and hear it is difficult to go on to the next stage of adapting it to suit us.

So it is with children. Imitative play comes first, then later it is embellished by their imagination in a variety of ways to suit their needs. As they grow up they continually watch and copy because that is the rewarding pattern we have laid down for them – copying is perhaps *the* most basic learning process in both man and animals – and they use it to the full as they watch other people doing things they may not see at home, or doing familiar things in an unfamiliar way, and copy again and again to the best of their growing ability.

One day I looked out of the window and saw our four-year-old son standing under the cherry tree with a short stick held between his first finger and thumb, with his other fingers curled tightly in his palm. He put the stick between his lips held it there for a few seconds, then put his hand behind his back palm up, threw his head back, pursed his lips and blew out. He repeated this slowly and deliberately several times before throwing his 'cigarette' to the ground and grinding it under his heel. Only one man on the farm smoked in precisely that way, and extinguished his cigarette with the safety of farm buildings and strawstacks uppermost in mind.

I shall never know when the moment came for Simon to register the cigarette-smoking as a separate part of the general image of this particular man, or whether he had practised it before. My guess is that he suddenly 'saw' this vaguely familiar ritual in sharp focus, came up the path with it still vividly in mind, went to the cherry tree to snap off the brittle tip of a low branch, and carried out the sequence of events precisely as he had just registered them.

I never saw it happen again and the chances are that having gone through all the motions he 'knew' how it felt to be that particular man smoking a cigarette, and was satisfied. The only time he might have repeated it was during one of the children's endless games of 'Doe's Men', when their makeshift tractor or harvester would break down and one was dispatched to phone Doe for a repair van to come out, while another tinkered with the 'engine', and the foreman (smoking his cigarette) would redeploy the men on different jobs until the repair job had been done.

Our daughter loved the cows more than the machinery, so her copying centred on the cowman – but we found her once lying on her tummy licking the cowshed saucer of cats' milk with her tongue to see what it felt like to be a cat.

I remember watching a child in a dark and gloomy church-hall playgroup in Plymouth in which the oppressive surroundings were offset by the beauty and imagination of all that was on offer. A little girl with golden shoulder-length hair was standing in front of a low mirror trying on hats from a box brimming over with a wide assortment of immaculate beauties. She tried several, then she found a short bridal veil, with pearl-spangled tulle springing from a headband. She put it on, and magic enveloped her. She gazed at her reflection with wide-eyed wonder – and became her mother. She put up one hand to run through her hair, lifting it at the temple and stroking it down along her jawline and under her chin. She turned her head this way and that, tilting her face up and to one side, and patting and stroking her hair into place. She was enchanting, and giving every indication that she was, in the words of the advertisement, preparing to be a beautiful lady.

I asked the supervisor if the child's mother was a grown-up version of her daughter, and she said 'Yes she is lovely in every way, beautiful to look at and a lovely mother – in fact it is a lovely family.' I asked if she had made the veil and she said 'Yes. Children so love pretty things. I bought a pearl necklace at Woolworth's, unthreaded it, and sewed the pearls on separately – the children love it, the boys as much as the girls.'

It isn't just the clothes children try on, it is the feelings that the clothes induce, for children are highly responsive to colour and materials. Often a timid child can be bold protected by a long dark cape, and peering at the world from under a dark wide-brimmed hat pulled well down over the eyebrows. Or stolid and clumsy children can enjoy a feeling of lightness and brightness enveloped in billowing pink tulle, and I have watched a real tearaway don majesty with a crown and fur-fabric-trimmed cloak.

If children are offered only one pattern, to which they conform, it narrows their choice and adaptability for the future. They may come to say 'I couldn't bear to dress up, I'm a jeans person' or 'I don't know how women can go round in trousers all the time', when what they really mean is 'I only ever dress like this because that's what we do in our family. I don't know what it feels like to dress any other way . . . and I don't want to try. I'm happy as I am.' And what *that* often means is 'I don't want to risk anything new in case I make a mistake . . . in case I don't know what to do . . . in case I feel at a disadvantage . . . in case I feel unsure instead of comfortably certain.'

If this applies to ways of dressing, think how it affects attitudes of mind – 'I call a spade a spade, I can't be doing with all that sensitivity' or 'I didn't like to say anything, you can't hurt people's feelings, can you?' Things are rarely black or white, and we all need help in finding our way through the grey areas in between the extremes.

Some years ago two of us made three ten-minute films in a playgroup in Bracknell, chosen because of the richness of the play materials but also because the adults in this group had a wonderful quality of stillness. Instead of being on top of the children they submerged themselves so the children really were free to play – and it *was* freedom they had, not licence. The calm and loving adults were physically, but not mentally, still. They watched and learned from the children all the time, and went on bringing in props and materials to extend the play they saw evolving.

We made one film in the large home-corner, having

spent one morning watching before we filmed. One adult was almost part of the furniture, being whatever the children wanted her to be without curbing their imaginative play in any way. They were so absorbed and busy that no interference was necessary.

In the bedroom section a home-made dressing-table covered with rose-patterned draperies had a real mirror, brushes and combs, curlers, dummy lipsticks (supplied by the local chemist's shop when the display colours were out of date), a powder puff and empty powder box, empty tubes and pots that had contained creams and empty nail varnish pots. During the course of the morning both boys and girls used the adult and each other to practise hair-brushing and the putting in of curlers – they soon discovered that the adult sat still longer than the children when it came to the intricate business of inserting rollers, and the even harder art of securing them in place with hairpins.

The child with long hair knew exactly how to brush the long hair of her friends, holding one tress up while the brush stroked it underneath from the roots to the tip. But that didn't work on short hair, so she watched the other children and copied what they did.

No one said a word. Words would have got in the way because the children were operating at a deeper level, carrying in their minds the bedrooms and bathrooms at home and reproducing what went on there here in the playgroup.

Carrying images in one's mind effectively is a very difficult thing to do and the skill has to be learned. It can be if we don't interfere with words too soon. A child who managed eventually to twist hair round a roller was mystified when she let go and it unrolled itself again. She persevered, getting quite good at the rolling operation, which boosted her confidence and helped to cushion her disappointment when it all fell down again. But eventually her attention was focused on the final outcome and she said 'Why won't it stay up?' and only then did the adult hand her a hairpin saying 'See if this will help.'

We watched both boys and girls trying to put rollers in each other's hair, and it was salutary to be reminded that the children had to discover by trial and error that rollers won't work on very short hair. It is pointless to offer them our knowledge at this stage, for real learning comes from doing, not being told. They might have believed us and not tried to roll up Tom's crew cut, but that would have denied them the surprise, bewilderment and satisfaction of finding out for themselves. Children feel a sense of mastery in learning by trial and error – the same sense of mastery that we so often feel in telling them not-to or how-to.

We watched both boys and girls applying imaginary lipstick with wonderful precision mimicking their mothers. Some stretched their top lip taut over their teeth as they traced the outline and then filled it in. Some parted their lips and dabbed the lipstick on. Some applied it in firm strokes from the centre outwards – and one child put the lipstick down, curled her third finger behind her little finger and used it, thus stiffened and steadied, to blend the imaginary colour into her lips. They 'were' their mothers.

They were just as sure about how their mothers used powder. Some shut their eyes, some dabbed lightly, some blotted, some stretched down their top lips and took great care to work the puff into the crevices on each side of the nostrils, some finished with light downward strokes. They were equally sure about men using a razor, and one used the wrong end of a lipstick like a styptic pencil to staunch an imaginary cut.

This copying is immensely important; apart from anything else is shows that they are still interested and alert, wanting to copy and learn how to master new skills as well as wanting to 'feel' what it is like to be the people who do all these things. But if we only see what they are doing to our belongings, and object, then eventually we blunt their desire to look, learn and copy – if the imitative play through which they learn almost always earns disapproval, why carry on?

On the other hand, cosmetics are expensive, razor blades are sharp, and parents can't always be expected to give their children a free hand. Once we understand how important this type of play is in the lifelong scheme of learning then it becomes a happy habit to look before anything is thrown away. Whether it is a bladeless razor, an empty after-shave bottle or roll-on deodorant, a finished lipstick, a discarded wallet or handbag, an empty box or tin, the clips from a new shirt, the cardboard cylinder from a roll of plastic bags, cling foil or baking foil, the bow from a chocolate box or bouquet – whatever it is, we can say 'Would you like this, or shall we throw it away?' If we give them both opportunity and permission to use the discarded symbols of our grown-up lives they benefit twice over – by feeling free to play and by being able to go through all the motions of the acts safely. They can learn to powder without getting it in their eyes, to apply after-shave without getting wet, to shave without getting cut. Their imaginations are so vivid that they don't need visible proof that they are doing all these things. The object of this particular stage of play is to feel what it is like to be someone else rather than to experience the outward sensations of these activities on oneself.

One of the natural invitations to copy comes from television advertisements. Advertisers are, I think, wide of the mark when they show children eating with abominable table manners. Most parents mind very much indeed about table manners and their anxiety already causes upsets at meal times, but the advertisements provide children with the perfect answer. They can do what they are forbidden to do with the safety net of 'But I'm only pretending to be the children in the advert – and *their* parents just laugh and give them some more!'

Imitative and imaginative play is often used as a safe way of doing what is forbidden – and as such it is valuable, particularly as an outlet for aggression. But advertisements that distort family life are a disservice to both children and parents, and the manipulative element detracts from the innocence that characterises imaginative play.

Sometimes children reproduce an action accurately, but at an inappropriate time or in an inappropriate place or way – like the children who know how to pick a bunch of flowers and the pleasure they will give but aren't yet sure about the property distinctions of fields, hedgerows, churchyards, parks and other people's gardens; or knowing that soap is necessary for a good wash, but not knowing when plain water is enough.

We need to treat these mistakes gently, neither by

excessive censure nor by laughing when we tell other people about them in the child's presence. Many a grown man or women trying to learn to cook will testify to the distress of having failures laughed at in a way that makes them feel diminished – though laughing-with can sometimes be comforting.

As children move outwards from the home they meet new people and experiences and, given the time to watch long enough, they will begin to copy these, too. To understand how much time they need we must remember how much time *we* need to learn something completely new.

I can remember watching the teacher work out a division sum on the blackboard, which she then rubbed out and did again from the beginning. Then she rubbed that out, too, and put the first line up again, saying 'What happens next?' People called out, and the sum was completed a third time. Yet again she chalked up the first line and said 'Who will come and work it out?' One of the quick ones did it in a flash, and then the sum was written up for the last time, we were told to copy it down in our books, and the blackboard was cleaned.

I sat there and panicked. Then I looked up at the empty blackboard and I could 'see' the first step, so I looked down and did it in my book. I looked back to the board and 'saw' what she did next, so I looked down and did that too – and so it went on.

Finally I got it right, and the next sum I did by referring to my first one without needing the blackboard. I know from sharing this experience that many others have had to go through exactly the same sequence of events – but without sufficient exposure to whatever it was we were trying to learn we would have been lost.

So it is with children who are trying to learn something at the stage when they still don't understand what they see. They need one very long exposure to someone doing a job – such as filling up a tank with petrol – or a great many short exposures before the sequence of events is clear enough in their minds for it to be reproduced in play.

The father of a grown-up family remembers the weekly ritual of his father pumping up the tyres, checking the brakes, and oiling the family bikes before he took the older boys for their weekly spin on Sunday afternoons. As he was only about five at the time he wasn't one of the cyclists, but he took enormous pleasure and pride in pretend-oiling the bikes and helping to get them ready.

It pays to plan walks or shopping expeditions with watching-time built in, with high priority to anything unexpected such as a pneumatic drill breaking up the surface of the road. I have seen a child reproduce this with amazing accuracy using a rolling pin. He tried with sticks jabbing into the ground but it didn't satisfy him, so he found the rolling pin, clutched the smooth polished handles and imagined the spike. He found this gave him the feeling he wanted of juddering both arms, then heaving the imaginary weight up and plonking it down on the next patch of path before juddering (with appropriate noises) all over again. The fact that no impression was made on the path didn't bother him in the least; he was much more interested in feeling what it felt like to 'be' the man.

You could, of course, allow time for ten boys and ten girls all to watch the same operation only to find that some weren't interested, some didn't like the noise, some were interested at the time but didn't want to follow it up in their play, whilst a few – boys or girls – did want to play it out afterwards. There should be no attempts at guiding children's choice. They should all be free to look, learn and replay what interests them in their own way, and the bonus for parents is that their own imagination will be quickened as they try to spot the work going on around them that children may not have seen in close-up before.

Chapter 13

'How does it feel
to be . . . ?'

Imitative play is an attempt to find out how it feels to be someone else by doing what they do, but because it is founded on observation children sometimes reach a dead end in the middle of their play because they haven't seen the next bit of action.

At a very simple level this can be seen in a home-corner when the one who has chosen to be Dad gets up and has a shower or sticks his head under the tap, sits down to breakfast or eats his pretend toast as he shaves, grabs his lunch-box or his brief-case and announces 'I'm off to work. Goodbye, see you this evening' and goes out of the door. But once outside indecision sets in – what is 'going to work'? A surprising number of children think that their fathers work at the railway station because that is where they are dropped each morning. Others know that their fathers work in a factory or office – but what goes on in a factory or office? There is nothing to copy, and often the child will wander around for a bit and start doing something else, or else walk purposefully around the room a couple of times trying not to lose steam before bursting into the home again with 'I'm back! What's for tea?'

A little girl not yet four went alone into the home-corner, stood by the telephone and carefully arranged herself so that one foot was crossed over the other with her toecap resting on the ground and the back of her left hand was on her hip. Wobbling slightly, she picked up the receiver of the telephone and tried to dial with her first finger. It was too difficult. She put the receiver down, dialled a number, picked up the receiver again and waited. Then she said 'Hello, is that you? It's me! For God's sake come round and have a sherry. I'm bored, bored, bored!' and as she said the last three words she tapped her toecap on the floor in unison. Her powers of observation were remarkable, but at the end of it there was a sense of flatness because having said the magic words she wasn't any further forward. She knew how it felt physically to be her mother doing all that, but it hadn't given her a clue as to how she had 'felt' making that phone call. Boredom and sherry were outside her experience.

Sometimes children will reproduce more familiar episodes that show real experience of their family pattern. There is a delightful sequence in the home-play film* I mentioned earlier where a tiny child is a happy, purposeful mother in miniature. She puts her baby in the high chair, bustles about preparing food and scrapes the contents of a bowl into a dish – going back to give one last scrape round the bottom of the bowl as she turns it over and gives it a little shake. She tucks the baby into bed, and when Dad comes home enters easily into the spirit of his family pattern as they carefully toss the baby to each other and hug it.

Someone has to cook the meals and, whether it is the mother, father, au pair or granny, I only hope that more and more children learn by their example to go about it this happily, combining chores and children into the real art of homemaking. Their children will then have a flying start with a strong and loving pattern of homemaking behind them.

Other children reproduce their own patterns only to find that they differ from other people's. A small solid boy was ironing one day, smoothing the garments on the board, spitting on the bottom of the iron to test it for heat, ironing both sides of the hair ribbons, and putting a cloth over a knitted baby jacket before pressing it lightly. Then the garments were carefully folded and hung over the clothes-horse at this side. A rather bossy little girl came in, looked at him and said 'Daddies don't iron!' The little boy said 'Mine does' and then stopped with the iron in mid-air to think for a bit before saying 'when there's a baby in the house.' He wasn't making excuses or being apologetic – it seemed as though it had just struck him that there was a time when

* *Children and Homeplay*, one of a series of nine 10-minute films made by I. E. Films Ltd in conjunction with the Pre-school Playgroups Association.

Dad didn't iron ... so when did it start? Then he knew. But, clearly, watching his mother iron had been a peaceful and happy experience. And the chances are that he will continue to iron when the need arises throughout his life. What is more, he will iron well and may actually enjoy it.

Another child, Charles, embarked upon a copycat exercise which may lead to an unexpected outcome one of these days. He was the very large child of a very large and forceful mother and a very small and subdued father, and one day he had clambered into the rest bed with its pillows, sheets and blankets but couldn't make himself comfortable. With great precision he stretched out, clasped his hands behind his head and shouted 'Richard, fetch me a pillow.' This first time he got the response he expected because another child brought it to him and helped to put it in the right position. All highly satisfactory to them both – he loved being waited on and she loved waiting on him. There is *nothing* wrong with this as long as it isn't the only pattern for both of them for the rest of their lives.

The day will probably come when he issues his order yet again and a child from a differently managed family turns his or her back saying 'Fetch it yourself!' Charles will then be very surprised, and possibly angry or sulky, but he will be faced with the fact that issuing orders doesn't always work, and during subsequent play episodes he will have a chance to work out various ways of coping with the problem. It is right here at the level of spontaneous play that children begin to learn about family patterns, and to feel their way forwards by trial and error – learning about flexibility, manipulation, domination, giving in and sticking out, and generally experimenting with relationships and attitudes as they play with each other.

One day when we were filming in a different playgroup a joyless little four-year-old girl went into the home-corner, which had been left a shambles by a group of boys. She stood in the doorway surveying the scene, arms akimbo, then she shook her head, heaved a sigh, and moved in to clear up. She picked up chairs, hung up clothes, gathered the stack of plastic plates, cups and saucers from the floor and table and began to wash them up in an imaginary bowl of water. Every plate was 'washed' and dried back and front, and the pile was patted into a smooth stack. Then she wiped her hands, folded her arms, and surveyed the scene again. It was touching and sad, and I said to the playgroup leader 'Tell me about little Granny.' She replied 'Just that. She is illegitimate and her mother has left home so her grandmother looks after her. She is loving and good but very old and tired.' Unless this child can be exposed to happy and buoyant homemaking she may well grow up to know, and do, her 'duty' in the home with uncomplaining joylessness – and what a travesty of motherhood, wifehood and homeliness that would be.

Sometimes children from widely different social backgrounds will play together in perfect harmony, divided sharply in detail but at one where it matters. Two such children attended the same playgroup, one whose parents moved in diplomatic circles, the other from the tenement block of flats which had prompted the starting of the playgroup in the first place. The child from the flats stirring cotton reels in a large saucepan with a wooden spoon said to her companion 'I'm making the stoo for dinner.' The other replied 'All right, while you do that I'll just pop to Harrods for the canapés.' It didn't matter in the least to either of them that one child was used to scrag-end of mutton and the other to smoked salmon. Where they were united was in their understanding that each was being responsible in her own way for feeding the family.

The more we all agree on fundamentals the less superficial differences matter. Giving birth and caring for the family in its formative years is of fundamental importance, and the attitudes of heart and mind towards all that this entails are infinitely more important than whether we have milk bottles or jugs on the table. It is often in play that children first begin to meet and mingle their lifestyles, and to learn from each other by trial and error as well as copying.

Children accept what happens at home. They may not always like it, and some of the patterns they follow are less happy and creative than they might be, but for each and every child 'home' is special and their parents are *their* parents and matter more than anyone else in the world.

Parents, like their children, need the opportunity to 'play' with each other so they too can be exposed to new patterns – and this is why the playgroup movement is so important. When parents themselves run playgroups they all have a chance to be exposed to children playing, and over the years they've been saying to me ruefully 'You don't know what you're like until the children imitate you. You can't help laughing, but it hurts a bit at times. Still, at least you can do something about it if you know.'

Some of the examples they have given stay in my mind, like the pair squabbling about who was going to be mother and father (sex doesn't come into this, boys and girls want to try out both roles). Finally one said 'You be Daddy and bring home the sweets, and I'll be Mummy and stay at home and shout.' This led to the exchange of some heartfelt comments between the mothers, many of whom have mixed feelings – fathers usually see less of their children and can sometimes feel jealous of the close mother–child bond, and so try to strengthen their own relationship by being what a mother described as 'the blue-eyed boy' when they come home. Other mothers want the fathers to be close, and don't mind how they express this desire to the child. Some mothers resent the fact that they have to be the disciplinarian because the father comes into the category of a 'treat' and doesn't want to spoil this image or always be an 'ogre' as soon as he comes home. Some fathers feel they have been working all day and deserve peace and quiet when they come home, or never really feel that being at home all day is 'work'.

There are endless variations on this theme, but the whole point is that these feelings wouldn't have been brought to the surface and shared if one mother hadn't heard this comment from the playing children and used it as the starting-point of a valuable discussion. And until mothers have discussed it, and sometimes modified their own feelings, they are not in a position to go home and talk about it if they want to and are able. They can also go home and play at copycats themselves as they change tactics to try out someone else's pattern in the privacy of their homes.

Another very common scene in the home-corner is for

a 'mother' or 'father' to nag, grumble and slap. This is shocking to some children, who may be unable to express any of their own aggression because their family pattern is almost unnaturally controlled and peaceful. But they copy, and although they have never hit or been hit at home they may delight in smacking the dolls, shaking them, throwing them down and knocking their heads together. The last thing these children want is someone breaking up their play with 'Now stop it, we don't treat our dolls like that. Pick them up. Now play nicely. If you can't behave properly you will have to come out of the Wendy House' or 'Poor dolly! What ever are you doing to her? You're the last person I expected to see being unkind. Give her a kiss.' These reactions tell children that we don't understand them.

Children, particularly over-controlled children, *need* to feel and release the aggression that is a right and proper part of us all. The more it has been denied the more explosive it may be when it surfaces.

Playing at being a 'naughty' mother or father is a legitimate way of doing and saying things that are not allowed. There should always be some dolls and soft toys that can be ill-treated in this way for if the aggression is aimed at a specific object it is less likely to be aimed at another child.

Occasionally children vent their aggression on a 'best' doll or toy. Distressing as this may be for the parents and the donor of the gift, it is as well to think carefully before forbidding it or being upset. The choice of object is usually deliberate, and the purpose may be to punish the person who prizes it so highly. A parent, perhaps, buys an expensive toy which the child feels is a substitute for the time and attention which is what is longed for – so the toy is smashed as a way of saying 'I don't care about this stupid thing, I want you. And you've hurt me so now I'll pay you back, and I'll smash what you seem to value.' The unsaid, only dimly perceived, message may also be 'Stop telling me about how much money it cost, and that you go out to earn money to buy me lovely presents, because I don't want them. I'd rather have you.'

Many parents *have* to work, but never let a child feel that the reason for going away is to buy presents. It is easier for them to accept that it is of necessity for one reason or another. And tell them honestly what the reason is, even if they don't yet understand. Be particularly careful about buying presents if it helps to salve your conscience or helps you to square yourself in your neighbour's eyes. If you need to work, for one or more of many valid reasons, then go into it carefully and cover every eventuality that you can think of so that you are honest with yourself about your reasons.

Then accept that sometimes it won't work (nothing works all the time, neither devoting yourself totally to your child, nor part-time or full-time work), and that you will feel guilty or at least torn in two. At those times presents are totally irrelevant. Even if you live off bread and cheese instead of cooking for a while, and dust settles on every surface, what matters then is that your child has your attention – and that you are not too strained to give it.

Whether or not mothers go out to work there are inevitably periods when families come under pressure. Tiredness is usually a contributory factor, and the more tired and strained we become the more illogically certain we are that 'things must be done'. Leave them, and go to bed with your child for a read and a cuddle and a made-up story; then carry the child to his or her own bed and say that you will be going back to yours to see who goes to sleep first. And do it.

Sometimes in attacking a special toy children are punishing themselves, and this is rather more worrying if the message is 'I'm not worth much. I never get anything right. I never please anyone. I'm clumsy, silly, naughty, stupid . . . and I love this toy more than anything else in the world. But I'm no good . . . so I'll smash it up and then it will be no good either and we shall deserve each other.'

On the other hand it may just be smashed in a moment of general frustration or by accident – don't start to watch your child for problems. Just be content to watch children and listen to them in general, so that you heighten your own awareness.

One of the reassurances children need is that when their play takes them into a fantasy world, based on imitation and imagination, we approve of what they are doing and express this approval by joining in sometimes. Otherwise they can live in two separate worlds – our world and the world of their imagination, which is so real to them that they lose touch with ours at times. They need to pass from one world to the other with ease, and we can help just as surely as we can hinder.

A friend of mine recently had her four- and five-year-old grandchildren for the day following their return from holiday. They were full of the excitement of their experiences and as soon as they arrived asked if they could have dressing-up clothes. Vera found them hats, scarves, gloves, handbags and various other odds and ends. Then they asked for the button box, and carefully chose which buttons to put in their purses. Then they announced that it was time for them all to catch the bus, so the three of them sat one above the other on the stairs. The driver heaved and tugged at the heavy gears and large steering wheel of the 'bus', and fares were taken and change given. At one point Vera said 'And who are you today, have you got a name?' To which the reply was 'I'm Mrs Nobody.' 'And who am I?' To which the answer was 'You're my friend.'

Children love us to join in when we are asked. Our presence indicates understanding and approval, which in turn builds up a real friendship that knows no age barrier. What spoils it for them is for us to turn the play into an artificial lesson – 'How much is the ticket? If I give you *this* how much change will you have to give me?' The object of this particular bus ride was to re-create the holiday drive and driver, and the business of change would have got in the way of the images being recalled.

What confuses them is for us to enter their world and behave like a child rather than an invited guest.

Another grandmother told how she thought she would please two four-year-old boys by entering fully into their play. They had invited her to join them on their magic carpet and she allowed herself to get quite carried away saying 'Look at all the roofs down there, and the little fields . . . and I can see the sea!' The boys gave her a withering look and one said 'You must be barmy.'

Let the last word rest with Peter Ustinov, whose family

felt convinced when he was a child that he would make brummbrumm car noises for ever. His grandfather understood and said 'It's the noise of his imagination developing.' To which Ustinov himself added 'I wasn't *pretending* to be a car, I *was* a car ... and at night I backed into bed and turned off.'

Chapter 14

Healing Play

Play is the spur to happy, healthy growth and development. In their play children do what comes naturally, getting to know things and people by touching, testing, copying. They are endlessly doing things, being things, just being or bursting out in rhythm.

They go hunting for new experiences, explore the nature and limits of relationships, or create their own world where they replay again and again occurrences and feelings they haven't understood, haven't liked, or liked so much they want to repeat – just as it was or embellished by wishful thinking.

It is difficult to live our own lives so naturally. There are times when we are hurt, frightened, bewildered and temporarily bereft of our confidence and happiness. We are taken aback and even say we can't go on, or we manage to survive by reverting to a stage we probably thought we had outgrown. We may lash out at those who are nearest and dearest to us, take revenge, become self-centred and self-pitying, eat or drink too much, try to lessen the pain with tranquillisers – you name it, most of us do it if we are tested beyond our ability to cope.

At such times what we long for is someone who will understand, and has the time to listen as we talk – and talk, and talk. If we are the cause of an accident, even one as minor as breaking something we valued, we tell everyone how it happened as though to reassure ourselves that it really was an accident, that we couldn't have avoided it, that it wasn't our fault. Time restores perspective, but in the early stages we often need to talk it out of our system.

But what if we haven't got a friend who will listen, if we don't understand what is happening to us, if we can't even talk – what if we are children?

Children at least accept the ups and downs of life. Our expectations are less realistic: we almost feel that if only we try hard enough we should be able to make everything lovely for everybody.

Life can't be like that, especially family life. So often we overlook the fact that although it is possible to know suffering without love – and very embittering it can be – there is no way we can know love without suffering. Parents love their children, and children love their parents, and there is bound to be suffering of many kinds as the relationship changes. The total dependence of the child on the parents moves on through the tricky stages of the child's growing independence, towards interdependence and freedom – then full circle back again as parents depend more on their grown-up children, and may finally be totally dependent.

In addition to the difficulties of this fundamental relationship there are all the other loves to be experienced – and each child's attitude to all those other loves stems from the original experience of parental love.

Children who are secure in their parents' love can usually accept a new baby without undue stress and strain, or there may be a temporary bad patch while the whole family is brought low by disturbed nights and all that stems from being perpetually tired. But occasionally a child reacts badly, and things go from bad to worse. *This is nobody's fault*, but it is sometimes unfinished business from the youth of one parent or the other or both.

Imagine yourself back to the stage of falling head over heels in love for the first time, when you gave your 'self' without reservation, when your whole world revolved around the loved one – and the devastation when you were rejected for someone else. You probably didn't even see it coming, or grew apprehensive but tried to wheedle or coax your way back into your former position by doing, wearing, saying all the things that once gave pleasure to you both. And if that didn't work you may have tried a show-down, shouting and accusing, before rage turned to tears. You may have thrown back presents, or kept things which didn't belong to you – and if you still couldn't accept being jilted you may have made yourself a perpetual nuisance on the grounds that if you couldn't enjoy that relationship at least no one else would. Or you may have withdrawn from everyone and retreated inside yourself where no one could reach you. All this may sound 'childish', but that implies that we don't understand children. It is certainly childlike, and you may recognise the symptoms in children you have known who found difficulty in adjusting to the new baby in the family.

Think of it from children's point of view. They were the centre of everyone's attention, they had their parents all to themselves, they watched the lump under the maternity clothes and listened to explanations about what was happening now, and what would happen when it was time for the baby to be born. But none of it really registered, and the reality of a living, sleeping, crying baby must have come as a surprise if not a shock. Babies take so much time and attention, parents who are short of sleep can grow snappish, and there isn't always time to cuddle two children.

The older child begins to play up, going through all the stages you may have recognised during the break-up of a love affair.

The child wheedles and coaxes and tries to induce a repetition of happier times – but tired parents don't want a child to clamber in bed at 6 a.m. saying 'I've brought a book and I'll read you a story', neither do they want to be offered a pretend cup of tea and a leaf-and-mud sandwich when they are bathing the baby, nor do they think it adorable when their lipstick is used this second and less innocent time.

So, on to the show-down. The shouting of 'I hate you . . . I hate the baby . . . send it back', the defiant 'I shan't . . . I won't . . . I don't care', the stamping, banging, kicking rage against what is happening to the old way of life – before the screaming turns to tears of bewilderment and frustration.

Next stop, return some things, keep others. Throw the doll she gave me on the floor and break it – see if I care! Tear the stupid book, squeeze toothpaste over the bow-tie, chuck the racing car out of the window. And if the hurt inside still won't go away, then take her earrings and stuff them down the side of the chair, take her biscuits and stuff them inside me, take some money out of her purse, take her beads and give them to the girl next door. And if even that doesn't make me feel better then make sure her nice times with the baby are spoilt. Wait till it's being fed, then break something; wait till it's asleep, then wake it up; wait till it's being bathed, then grab the talc and run off with it.

The more impossible such a child's behaviour becomes, the less easy it is to express the love that is craved, and the more imaginative the child's attempts to regain love. Such children may refuse to drink from a cup and demand a bottle – they want to go back to babyhood themselves, to retreat to that golden age when they were the ones to be cuddled and fed. Play along with them, recognising that in distress we *all* want to go back to where we were before 'it' happened. If you can cuddle them and give them the bedtime bottle do. But if you are so fraught at this point that you can't, then do at least give the bottle freely and kindly with the goodnight kiss and tuck-in. And if the bottle is needed during the day give it, whilst recognising that the child won't want to give up the solace of babyplay until it becomes satisfying to be the bigger one. Praise (sincerely) anything that is remotely praiseworthy, and ask for help (sincerely) occasionally, but don't expect to win over quickly someone who feels so insecure.

These playing-up games are almost reflex actions, a sort of primitive survival instinct, but unless you can pick up the cues and supply what is needed they won't bring healing in themselves – though the bottle may bring comfort.

Resolving the jealousy may involve the use of legitimate violence, such as bashing and pinching a lump of dough with a fist or wooden spoon, or hammering nails into wood, or bashing the pegs of an outsize hammer toy. Once the inner rage is expressed and spent the play can continue for its own sake, bringing calm. And, when the moment comes for you both to meet in a moment of calmness, both of you will be reassured. If the relationship breaks down again don't despair, just find other play outlets to restore the equilibrium. Water may help, or a bowl of silver sand: the constant tipping and pouring and trickling through the fingers often soothes the senses and the inner turbulent feelings. But real peace won't be restored until and unless the child feels loved and secure. Contrary to what some people believe, it is seldom the children who are *certain* they are loved who react badly to a new baby. It is usually the children who have never felt quite sure that love was theirs unconditionally, or who have never felt quite sure that you knew where to draw the line and could control them when needed.

Children need love that doesn't have to be earned with quietness, goodness or cleverness; that isn't conditional upon fetching Mummy's hankie from upstairs, eating the cabbage, not coming in with dirty feet; that doesn't make unfavourable comparisons with Jane who could walk at a year, Tom who could talk at eighteen months, Sarah who could read at three, Peter who can stick up for himself, Megan who is so beautiful; that doesn't threaten withdrawal 'if you go on like this', 'if you don't do as I say'. They need to be loved for what they are and because they are ours.

But we are not perfect, and if we were not loved this much ourselves it takes time to learn to love freely – let alone wisely. And sometimes in spite of love something traumatic happens in a child's life that shakes even a sure foundation. It may be a death, or prolonged separation at a crucial time, or an accident of some sort. Or one or both parents may have problems of their own that affect their child, children, or one of their children. Whatever it is, a child may be particularly vulnerable, but even then may still find a way of playing that is enough to restore the health and integration of mind and body again.

Death is one such experience, and most children are fortunate enough to sense what the word means before they experience its impact. One mother wrote 'I remember sadness at death in the family – not really understanding it but feeling the unhappiness in my parents.'

A playgroup leader told of a local footballer being killed, and the streets being lined with mourners of all ages including schoolboys. It was the school's half-term holiday, and the next day one of the older brothers of a playgroup child came into the playgroup and began to organise all the children into a funeral procession. The children were delighted to respond to this big boy who had come to play with them, and, sensing his need and the children's complete lack of understanding beyond the game they were playing, the play leader didn't interfere. He tipped the bricks out of the box, replacing them with a doll, and announced it was the coffin that had to be taken very slowly in a car. So they put it on the wheeled trolley strewn with flowers from the vase. He organised the following 'cars', which children willingly rode. He arranged the ranks of mourners, and told them they had to stand very still and quiet while the coffin went by. Then he pulled the hearse himself, slowly round the playroom and through the door into the cloakroom, where he unloaded the coffin before pulling the empty hearse back into the hall. All this had taken a long time and by the time the procession had gone through the door the mourners had had enough, so they just drifted back to play in other ways. The boy, who had come into the playgroup quiet and strained, seemed relaxed and satisfied and was ready to join the mothers for tea and biscuits.

No one reminded him of the body in the cloakroom for they knew intuitively that he 'hadn't got there yet' – his personal involvement had been as part of a sombre crowd mourning a local hero, and that was the bit that he needed to replay in order to relieve the feeling of oppression that had stayed with him.

The mother of a grown-up family recalls that she used to play at being Mrs Wapson when she was little. 'My husband was always "very ill" – I don't know why, there was no illness or death in the family that I can see as I look back, but I can remember that I marked out a grave with stones, and put flowers and weeds on it and walked about feeling very grave and sombre.' Far from being morbid play it was play to rid herself of the morbid feeling imposed upon her by the special voices and demeanour of grown-ups referring to death in those days – much of which still remains.

Another mother in a group recalling early memories said 'We had a bay window with a wide window-seat round it, and long velvet curtains that pulled straight across. I used to love pulling the curtains and then playing in my private house behind them. Another thing I used to do was to dance about on the seat, playing at theatres I suppose. I can remember standing on the middle of the seat and feeling excited and important as I put my hands together where the curtains met, then I'd throw them back as far as my arms would let me and say "I'm here!" It felt marvellous.' Some weeks afterwards she wrote a letter:

'The memory I mentioned – about playing behind velvet curtains, the dusty smell and comfortable feel of them – has had a rather interesting follow-up!

'I have asked my aunt who I lived with for most of my childhood if she could remember having any such curtains or me playing behind them. She said it must have been in my first home but I could only have been about two-and-a-half or just three years old – she remembers I used to take my toys behind the curtains, which were floor-length and dark blue in colour, then pull them shut and play either on the floor or the low window-ledge which was very wide. It amazed her that I could remember it, as I must have been that young – my Mother died when I had just turned three, and I went to live with my grandparents almost immediately.

'Whilst talking about all this I mentioned how smells can make one *feel* for no apparent reason! I have always felt so very sad if I smell corn or straw or chicken smells! Aunt remembered at once: whilst I stayed with the grand-parents, who kept chickens, it used to worry them all that I would go off and sit in the run with the chickens usually holding a new egg, rocking and crying and talking to the hens. My grandmother had said to them "Leave her be to sit out her sorrow in her own way – it's God's way to heal."

'My aunt quoted it, just like that. She said she had not thought about it for years, but could see it now as if it were a few weeks ago.

'No one in the family had ever talked about my mother. They felt I had been too young to remember, so just didn't talk about her again. Now I've learnt so much more about her, I feel I know her as a person. I feel more complete.'

How lucky she was to have a grandmother who understood what those repeated visits to the hens were all about. She wouldn't have used the word 'play', but that is what I believe it was.

There are many definitions of play, none of which reveals the mystery at the heart of the experience. What matters is that we learn to recognise the significance *to them* of what children do – especially under stress – for they seem to have an inherent wisdom that is greater than ours.

In cases of extreme need it may take a sensitive and trained mind to offer opportunities for therapeutic play, together with the ability to interpret what transpires at each stage. Such an experience is recounted by Dr Virginia Axline in *Dibs: In Search of Self*,* a fascinating and readable account of a child, who, at five years old, was rapidly becoming classified as a defective but who eventually revealed himself to be a highly intelligent boy. This is one of the most popular books with playgroup parents who can see so clearly what has gone wrong, and what 'Miss A' (Dr Axline) is doing as she helps him to become a whole person.

I remember two-year-old Elizabeth during the war. Many children had been evacuated from London when the bombing started, but some parents decided to keep their youngest children with them – a decision some reversed after a particularly heavy raid in the Paddington area. At first light coaches were summoned, loaded with children from babies to three-year-olds and their bundles of clothing, and driven out to safe areas. Without their mothers.

Before the shock of the bombing and the journey had really registered one coachload of children found themselves in an ancestral mansion set in a deep park with a river running by. We discovered later that some of them didn't even know what grass was.

I was training at the Bedford Froebel Training College at the time, and those of us who were specialising in the nursery age were set to work to convert one of the lofty reception rooms into a playroom, and to staff it.

Elizabeth was shocked out of speech altogether. She was like a walking doll, going where she was led but standing or sitting as still as stone if her hand was released. There was no specialist help available and we had to do the best we could by observation and gut reaction.

* A Pelican book.

Eventually Elizabeth relaxed and would sit on our laps and watch the others, her eyes following them with some returning interest; then she began to walk about to find safe sitting-places with different views; then reach out for proffered toys, and hold them. Slowly she responded and began to play cautiously by herself or with one of us, but still not a word was uttered. The weeks and months went by and she started to talk a little and to play more purposefully, but still on her own unless someone came to join her, when she would respond to their lead. But she couldn't stand up for herself or cope with games that became boisterous. Then one day she threaded painted cotton reels on to a long pink lacing that we had extracted from a jumble sale corset of vast proportions and reinforcement – it must have been getting on for two metres. She surveyed the multicoloured result and, out of the blue, began to march purposefully round the room trailing it behind her and thrusting the metal tag towards everyone's face saying 'Snake!' They were all so surprised that they fell back a pace to look at it – and her – and before they had recovered she was on her way again.

I was sitting on a rug by the window and when it was my turn she said 'Snake! Eat you up!' I remember a split second in which I wondered how to respond. What had happened? What did she want? One look at her face was enough – she wanted to be big and confident and powerful. She'd had enough of being small, insecure and ineffectual. So I said 'No, no' or words to that effect, and backed away to cower by the radiator – and she followed, repeating 'Snake! Eat you up!' again and again. Then, triumphant but suddenly exhausted, she sat on my lap with Snake curling around us and his 'head' still in her hand.

From then on she couldn't be parted from Snake – it was as though she couldn't sort out which was Snake and which was her. Snake had given her the power she wanted but had lacked. If she let go, would she lose it? Better not let go in case! Besides, he was so useful as a buffer between her and things she wasn't sure about. If she was given unfamiliar food she could look at it, smell it, put Snake's nose in it, and say authoritatively 'Snake doesn't like it, he doesn't want any', and that was that. Easy. We obeyed

Snake in everything, though sometimes we said 'Do you think Snake would like a little bit of mine?' and occasionally he would and did. Then we would say 'Would you like to put a little bit on your plate for him?' and often that would work too. The other children were wonderful. It wasn't just that they enjoyed the game – if that was all they could have copied it. I am convinced that children can sense when another child is in trouble and will often rally round to be part of the healing process.

The one time Snake was a nuisance was on a walk. He would bounce and bump his way over gravel paths and lawns with no trouble but was literally a bind among the twigs, logs, long grass and brambles in the woods. Elizabeth's arm and shoulder grew so tired that his tail had to be carried, and even then the weight was considerable – and she only had one hand to pick up conkers.

We tried everything. Would Snake like to be tucked up in her bed while we were out? He nearly would, but at the last moment changed his mind. Would he like me to carry him? Emphatically no, for then (I suddenly saw) I would have the power and I already had more than enough. He had to come with us. But a chance remark – 'It's a pity he's quite so long' – found an echo in her own mind, and unobtrusively Snake grew shorter, and shorter, and shorter, until after several more weeks he was down to a single cotton reel in the pocket of her overall. But that was no ordinary cotton reel. It was the symbol that represented not only Snake in all his technicolour glory but also the totality of the experience built up around him.

With it she felt safe. Without it? That didn't bear thinking about at this point, so we all guarded it like the crown jewels.

She didn't need it often, but sometimes we would see her hand slip into her pocket for a reassuring touch – or even hover near her pocket at the ready, in case. But one day she really needed it. We had created three solid steps up to the top of an inverted tea-chest, and the children were queueing up on the grass to climb the steps and jump off the top. Elizabeth was among them and when her turn came she confidently mounted the steps, moved over to the far side of the top – and froze. Suddenly the ground looked a long way down, and we watched her coming to the moment of decision. Risk it and jump? No. Accept the outstretched hand offering help? She hovered then averted her eyes. Turn round and go back? Suddenly she remembered, put her hand in her pocket to retrieve Snake, and with complete composure said 'Snake doesn't want to jump today.'

I opened my mouth to say 'Snakes don't like jumping, do they?' but suddenly saw two things simultaneously: she didn't need me to make it easy for her to climb down those steps, she had managed it alone; and I would have blocked any renewed attempt to find the courage to jump later. If snakes 'don't like jumping' then next time she climbed those steps it would be assumed that *she* wanted to jump – and what if her courage failed again?

Symbols mustn't be divested of their power by other people. Some remain valid for life. Some are outgrown and forgotten. Others may be outgrown but linger in our memories, a source either of gratitude for the experience they stood for which remains part of the bedrock of our lives, or of distress if that experience fettered rather than liberated us.

Much of children's play is symbolic, and among their 'rubbish' there sometimes lurks an unremarkable object that is a symbol for something about which we know nothing. But it is precious to them and they need to keep it – rather as we keep the horseshoe off a piece of wedding-cake, a theatre ticket, a lock of hair or a shell picked up from last year's holiday. We attach sentiments to memories and may therefore keep our symbols longer, but theirs may be just as potent for them for the days or weeks of their importance.

There is no need to keep everything and treat it as a sacred relic – simply keep your eyes and ears open, and extend to children's property the respect you only wish they had for yours.

Chapter 15

'Cuddlies'

Many children are inseparable from a grubby piece of blanket, a one-eared rabbit, a length of satin ribbon or some other comforter which they trail around with them everywhere.

Unlike Snake, who became Elizabeth's go-between when she couldn't cope with the world in her own strength, 'cuddlies' are not a way of living at one remove. Rather they are a symbolic way of saying 'I should like my special protector to be with me all the time, but she (or he) is usually doing something else, so I'll manage by myself – with just a little something in my hand to keep me company.'

This is a step forward, not backwards. Put yourself in their place. You may be so used to carrying a handbag, shopping, a brief-case, or a transistor radio that if you haven't got it with you there can be a sudden momentary panic – 'I've lost it. Where did I leave it?' – before you adjust to the comfortable feeling that on this occasion you deliberately left it behind. In much the same way children are in the habit of having us with them, holding them in our arms, holding them by the hand or pushing them in a pram or buggy that is attached to us. When they first walk and begin to potter about the house we are always near at hand, usually in sight, and often still in personal contact. We are their total security, so no wonder they feel as if part of them is missing when they start to live more independently.

It is as they begin to realise that we are not part of them that they so often latch on to something that *can* be an almost inseparable part of them, a token substitute for us – a symbol that says 'I'm still with you even if you can't see me.'

I know twins, parents of schoolchildren now, who still remember the pieces of blanket they weren't allowed to take to school with them. They rushed home at the end of the first day and tore upstairs – but couldn't find them. They asked, and were told they had been washed and were on the line. So off they dashed into the garden only to find they were pegged out of reach. They sat on the ground sucking their thumbs with their eyes fixed on the precious objects until their mother restored them. And then – consternation – they didn't feel or smell right! They hadn't been washed before, and all the familiarity had been washed away to render them impersonal.

The first day at playgroup or school is the very day some children most want their comforters even if their mothers are with them – and even more urgently if they are not. Many parents are reluctant to allow this because they fear their children might be laughed at by bigger children, or might lose the precious object, which would create havoc at bedtime, or because they are secretly a bit ashamed that their child needs this 'babyish' comforter.

If you explain about the possibility of loss it sometimes helps to suggest that together you cut off a little piece of the comfort cloth just the right size to pin into a pocket with a safety pin. The pin will 'keep it safe', and it will be available for a quiet clutch every now and again if it is needed, without it being obvious to those who might tease. Remove it for washing but have it available in case it is asked for again, and the time will come when it is no longer missed.

I have a fellow feeling for these children because if when I stand up to speak at a meeting I suddenly realise that my handkerchief isn't with me I am completely thrown. I used to think that this was a rational anxiety since I could hardly wipe my nose on my sleeve if the need arose, but I have long since ceased to kid myself. My handkerchief is my comforter. It has to be tucked up my sleeve, or in my handbag on the chair behind me, with one corner sticking out between the clamped frame so that I can grab it quickly if I need to. I do the job without making a fuss, so why deny myself the feeling of safety this little piece of material gives me?

I find almost everybody I ask is slightly apprehensive about doing anything new for the first time, and about some things every time. This re-registered when our nineteen-year-old nephew was packing the night before leaving to work for a month as a night porter at a hotel in a French ski resort. He confessed 'I'm always a bit nervous at this point, though I know it will be all right when I get there'; and, much to his relief, his father said 'I know. So am I.'

So are almost all of us if we are honest with ourselves, and it will perhaps become easier to admit this when we understand that it is natural, not feeble. If we have any imagination we look ahead and see all the possible pitfalls as well as the pleasures of what we are about to do, so pause before making the final decision to go ahead. Then the adrenalin flows, we are keyed up for flight or fight if either is needed – and that carries us through to the triumphant moment when we say to ourselves 'I did it!' Or to those other moments when we have to admit 'I made a mess of that – but I still have two eyes a nose and a mouth, tomorrow will still be Wednesday, and I know what to do next time.'

If we never feel even a twinge of apprehension at the unknown, or if we conveniently overlook the fact or have never faced up to it, the chances are that we shall be unreasonably hard on our children. The more we deny our own fears the less self-awareness and confidence we have – and the more likely it is that we shall be particularly hard on them, wanting them not only to be more confident than we are, but more confident than is reasonable or even possible.

I remember a grandmother talking to me on a train. Her daughter and son-in-law had asked her to join them and their ten-year-old son on a package holiday abroad, an offer she had accepted with alacrity. She told me 'I spent the night before with them, and when I arrived they were having a bit of a set-to. My daughter had told her son to lay out on the bed everything he wanted to take with him – things to pack on one end, and things for the journey on the other. One of the things he wanted on the journey was an old rabbit he used to take everywhere with him as a child. My daughter looked at it and said "Well, you're not taking that for a start!" And he said he was, and she said he couldn't, and he said "What's the use of asking me what I want if you say I can't take it?" And she said "Well, I didn't think you'd want anything so daft – a great boy like you with a rabbit! What ever will people think of you?" And he said "I don't mind what they think of me, I want it."

'I felt sorry for the lad, because it stood to reason that he must have wanted it badly to risk looking so silly. So I said to him "Tell Grandma why you want it, love", and he said "Because I haven't been in an aeroplane before." Well, d'you know I was on his side, because I hadn't flown before and truth to tell I had a little drop of brandy in my handbag in case I needed it. So I said to my daughter "Let him take it if he wants to!" Well, the upshot of it was that he took it – and do you know, no one noticed it! Not a blessed one!'

How illogical we are about children. Many an RAF pilot in the last war took his original cuddlie with him in the cockpit. One pilot who did told us about the assortment of rabbits and bears, with or without their bows and woolly scarves, that were the treasured and flaunted possession of others. Only this time round they called them mascots.

No one can 'make' anyone else brave. Bravery isn't the absence of fear, but the courage to go ahead in spite of it. If we allow our children to know themselves and their limitations, to accept themselves, and to use childhood props when they need them, they are able to acquire the habit of facing the unknown. Nothing succeeds like success, and in their own time they outgrow the need for symbolic security.

But let it be in their time, and not for our face-saving.

Chapter 16

Imaginary Friends

We shared our home for several years with my sister's imaginary friends Acki, Buddy, Borslaw and Tatty.

I rather think I was midwife to the first one. Pauline was about three, I was two and a half years older, and we had reached the stage when we quarrelled and fought almost as often as we played together happily. On this occasion she took the wind out of my sails by ceasing hostilities with the dignified words 'Come on, Acki, let's go and play by ourselves'. Whereupon she disappeared under the dining-room table and proceeded to enjoy the company of someone who was so real that I can still remember feeling absolutely floored. Who was this person? She couldn't be real – or could she? Anyway, Acki won hands down. I wasn't to be included: Pauline was perfectly happy and engrossed, and I was left out.

Buddy and Tatty arrived at some point I don't remember, but the fourth one materialised in quite a different way.

We were having one of our rarest treats, tea in a shop. Our mother and aunt were with us, and we were looked after by a waitress in a brown dress with a cream apron and matching headband. We had cakes with cream in and powdered sugar on top, and ice cream in silver cups on stalks – I can recall the grandeur of the occasion still. At the end of the meal Pauline said 'Can I go and kiss Borslaw?' and she slid off her chair, went to the stout waitress, and put up her arms to kiss the elderly cheek bent down to her. Borslaw had joined the family.

I was powerless against this invisible army. I could swipe at them, offer bribes to join in, try to extent a helping hand to one or all of them – but to no avail. 'You didn't hit her, she jumped out of the way', 'They don't want any sherbet dabs, they've got their dinner', 'She can manage by herself', and – most crushing of all – 'We don't want to play with you, we're happy by ourselves.'

But ther were times when the two of us played happily for hours, washing dolls' clothes in the garden, cleaning out the potting shed that became our playhouse, having picnics and dolls' tea parties, but above all making mud pies. On these occasions either the 'friends' were forgotten or tagged along to the call 'Come on, we're going to make mud pies!' We were all aware of their reality and a cry of 'I can't go to bed yet, I've got to go and get Acki, Buddy, Borslaw and Tatty in from the garden' had to be met with a respectful 'All right, we'll go on up and you come when you've brought them in.' It worked. It was as though there was an unwritten bargain – 'You treat them as though they are real, and I won't take advantage of you.'

Only once do I remember them holding our entire family to ransom. We were all ready to go on holiday. The suitcases were in the car boot, the picnic baskets, shrimping nets, buckets and spades, bottles of water, kettle, primus stove and all four of us were in the car. My father said his usual moving-off speech – 'Right, we're off! Everybody got everything?' – and there was an agonised cry of 'No! Acki isn't here.'

There was nothing for it but to let Pauline out of the car, and watch her go back up the path, round the bay window, along the lavender hedge and disappear from view. No one said anything. We just waited. Quite soon she came back with her usual quiet dignity and said 'I've found her!' Then she clambered in, settled down and off we went.

That was the last time I remember the quartet. If it really was the last time, it may have been because she had tested us all as far as she needed to go, or because she felt she could speak up for herself from then on or, because the change of scene for a fortnight hot on that last triumph gave her the opportunity to let go of an idea that was becoming more of a burden than a refuge. But they are still remembered with affection by us all.

Although imaginary friends arrive out of the blue, sometimes they depart less easily. One mother recounted how her younger daughter suddenly produced Maggie, a 'child' so real that she became not only part of the family but part of the neighbourhood. Her imaginary pram was pushed faithfully wherever they went, the handle clutched tightly in outstretched hands. It was bumped up and down the kerb, the brake was applied and released at each stop outside a shop, and Maggie was tenderly lifted out and carried in. Even the bus conductors knew her and would get down from the platform saying 'Want a hand with Maggie's pram?' and would lift it up to stow it carefully under the stairs, lifting it down again at the journey's end.

Time went by, then one day the family was driving over the Severn bridge when there was a cry of 'Maggie's fallen out!' There were offers to stop to look for her, but apparently it 'wouldn't be any good', so they went on their way. The day wore on and the child became quieter and quieter. Then, as they drove home and were recrossing the bridge, the tension broke with 'It's all right! Maggie's just hopped up on to the luggage rack!'

It had taken this child the whole day to discover that she wasn't yet ready to dispose of Maggie, so she was brought back to life. Maggie eventually faded away, but was briefly resurrected during a visit to hospital for the removal of tonsils when the child was about seven.

Another mother recalled her son's inseparable companion – I forget his name but we'll call him Arthur – and remembered well when he was finally relinquished. She was busy in her kitchen when her son came in, slightly subdued, to say bluntly 'Arthur's dead.' She played safe by saying in a non-committal tone of voice 'Is he?' and was rewarded with a further snippet of information – 'He was run over by a car and killed.' Still trying to find a tone of voice that would show she was with him without probing or offering a lead of any kind, she said 'Well!' and the next observation, 'I've buried him in the dustbin', rated an 'Ah!'

She had the feeling he was making it up as he went along, trying to see how he felt about one stage before going on to the next. He seemed satisfied, didn't offer any further comments, and ran off to play.

After a while he returned looking happy and relaxed, and with radiant certainty he rounded off Arthur's valuable and happy life with 'It was a sports car that killed him. A beautiful *yellow* sports car!'

It is easy enough to explain imaginary friends in terms of companions for lonely children, as reinforcement for children dominated by other members of the family or as a substitute for tangible cuddlies – all of which they may be. But that is only our adult reasoning and doesn't take into account how much these 'friends' do for children in their own right.

For years I have watched and listened to children engaged in conversation and play with their 'friends'. Some characteristics remain constant. Above all, the children are happy, confident in the relationship and about what they are going to do – even if it is saying 'Come on! Let's get out of her way', then standing on the landing chuntering quietly without doing anything while they gather themselves together.

Much of their time together is engaged in quiet chat, with smiles and chuckles of sheer pleasure. Sometimes there is verbal or physical aggression towards these imaginary friends or children, but the release of pouring it all out brings peace and reconciliation. It is as though there is a stage when bashing dough or hammering nails is no longer enough to restore inner harmony, as though a personal relationship is needed. Perhaps this form of play foreshadows the need we all feel to find someone with whom we can be fully ourselves in all our moods, without the overall balance being tipped towards dominance or subservience – and sometimes only an imaginary person can meet this need at what may be a rehearsal stage for later living.

In their play these children will also experiment with events, replaying something that has happened and giving it an alternative outcome – in this way they can explore new situations in privacy and with safety or rehearse a new option before trying it out.

Confession is another element in their play. If their courage is not yet as strong as their desire to own up and put things right, well, one's best friend can be relied upon for a sympathetic hearing and understanding. One's best friend can also most conveniently be blamed! If this happens, use the imaginary friend to let your child know what the outcome would have been in the event of a direct owning up. If you say 'Oh, no she didn't. You did it, and don't try to get out of it' your child will feel the need to hide the evidence next time rather than face such intimidating anger. If you say 'It's a pity about the milk all over the floor, but I'm sure it was an accident. Do you think you could help Lulu mop it up?', then you have made it possible for the wrong to be righted and paved the way for making a clean breast of it next time – which is much more important than holding an inquest about milk that is already spilt.

Parents sometimes worry about the danger of pretending to believe in someone or something that isn't real, but I feel sure children know deep down that we are aware of what is going on and are grateful that we have offered them a way out that will make next time easier. I believe our ability to move in and out of their fantasies reassures them that such movement is possible and that we understand and approve.

After all, we do it too. We wash the dishes or the car and fantasise about being showered with bouquets after a star performance, inventing something which would bring us a fortune, sailing away from it all with the impossibly perfect companion. In these daydreams our real lives are only suspended – or if we temporarily kill off our nearest and dearest it is with the childlike certainty that we can bring them back to life again when the dream is over!

We all need our daydreams and fantasies, for although it *can* lead to a Walter Mitty life it doesn't have to. Walter Mitty lived so deeply immersed in his imaginary roles that he couldn't distinguish fantasy from reality.

I remember an eleven-year-old at the child guidance clinic who was unable to read and said 'Frankly, there's no point in it – the books in the library aren't worth reading. I'm going to make my mark in electronics and I know more than they can tell me now. I've wired up a system at home that means I can contact my parents outside and in.' He had, too. I was invited to his home and met his excessively proud and adoring father, who was a retired Royal Navy captain.

He was a highly intelligent child, and his father had taught him lovingly and well. The trouble came when he went to school, was treated as 'one of the little ones', and didn't count as an adult among adults. The shock was great, especially when he discovered that some of 'the children' could already do things he couldn't do – and he didn't dare try in case he fell below his image of himself as being his father's equal. Though based on a foundation of solid achievement, his fantasies had divorced him from some fundamental realities. The gap was bridged and he made up the missed learning stages amazingly quickly once he decided that it was also a sign of manliness to admit what he didn't know.

Other children without parents to give them a legitimate if exaggerated feeling of self-worth fare less well. They can opt out and live in a dream world of their own – though most opt in again when they are ready. In adult society like-minded people whose private world centres on values that are vicious, greedy and perverted sometimes gang together. Similarly, those whose world is idealistic and peace-loving may retreat to set up a commune or spiritual community of their own. In either of these groups some will come back to the mainstream of society feeling wiser than before, while others will continue with their chosen way of life in which they feel at home.

There is much discussion nowadays whether or not violence and pornography feed the fantasies of those who have insufficient access to other values to be able to withstand or counter them. But there is also speculation that the positive value of daydreams and fantasies may have been underrated – a feeling to which I subscribe. I believe we need this form of interior living as an integral part of our lives. Children may have much to teach us about this. They live out their fantasies, and are therefore in a better position than we are to test them against reality. We may not bring our two separate lives together, preferring to retreat from the outer to the inner in order to maintain a tolerable balance.

But if we can learn to use our inner escapism to help us *do* something about whatever it is that we are trying to escape from or resolve, then it can be a powerful force in helping us to go on growing up.

Chapter 17

Toys

Toys are the tools of play in much the same way that trowels, hoes and secateurs are the tools of gardening. The possession of toys doesn't guarantee a flourishing play experience any more than gardening tools guarantee a flourishing garden. But with inclination, time and opportunity tools can be an asset – providing they are well chosen and looked after.

No matter how carefully you choose toys, some are never really enjoyed whilst others assume a personal importance out of all proportion to their cost. And sometimes a toy has a particular value because it was specially made for a child or the child helped in the making.

Children are individuals and can prove us wrong as often as right. Our son's first favourite toy was a sponge-rubber goldfish about eight inches long. The next was a stout wooden trolley, a present for his third birthday, which carried grass cuttings, bricks, windfall apples, other children and picnics for years. Then at four he inherited a Meccano set that so fascinated his fingers and fired his imagination it started a lifelong interest which eventually led to mechanical engineering as a career.

Our daughter had but one great love, a small bear which was cuddled threadbare and was part of her luggage wherever she went until she was in her teens. We really pushed the boat out for her third birthday and made a pram from a stout apple-box – we spent hours on the construction and sandpapering and painted it with flowers and butterflies, then made all the bedding and dressed a doll. *We* had a marvellous time but she hardly glanced at it and only used it once, when it became the bed for three farmyard kittens after their mother was killed. She only ever wanted to be with the animals or busy with her own pursuits, endlessly doing things with no time to spare for anything else.

One of my own favourite playthings was a doll, Princess Moonshine Short for Bubbles. My sister's favourites were a miscellaneous collection of stuffed animals. But our real love was an ever-growing collection of little lead farm animals which we played with for years. We made farmhouses and barns from Swiss-roll boxes thatched with sheets of paper scribbled yellow, folded over and stuck along the top. The animals' pens were little boxes fenced round with matchsticks stuck in plasticine. Hedges evolved from twigs stuck in small mudbanks. Trees were larger twigs stuck in cotton reels. Grass cuttings dried in the airing cupboard became hay in the fields, to be raked up with a broken comb and made into haystacks and animal bedding. Peas were potatoes to be planted, then harvested and stored in earth clamps with straw to keep them from the frost. Sultanas were animal-droppings cleared out of the stable and cowsheds, carted to the dungheap, then later spread over the fields before being ploughed in.

The farm covered a wide windowsill along one side of our bedroom in winter, and would be taken into the garden during the summer – reassembled every day since we couldn't bear to leave it outside all night. We held auctions, went to market, bought and sold, suffered the ravages of swine fever and foot-and-mouth, became vets, rescued animals from the muddy dyke, and broke off at intervals to make or improvise some other extension to further the play. It was about the only time we never quarrelled, and on looking back I suppose it was because we weren't us; we *were* Charlie, Cooty, Owen and all the other people whose parts we played.

My mother remembers a doll's pram with a white china handle in which she took her rabbit, cat and dog for endless rides. Her sister's stand-by was a small dumbell on a piece of string which was her dog.

My publisher's pride and joy was a large red pedal racing-car in which he drove races round Silverstone or Brands Hatch.

Try to recall your own special toys, and look at your own and other people's children. See which toys are personal treasures, which are passing interests and which ones lend themselves to infinite variations of play, as did that trolley and the farm animals.

The range of toys is now so extensive that choice is difficult, but before you buy there are some general points to bear in mind.

Is it a case of the more toys the better?

No, for this would be like saying the more clothes the better – you could end up with cupboards full of clothes and still feel you have nothing to wear. It is often the child with cupboards full of toys who says 'I've got nothing to play with.'

Bear in mind the following points:

1 If children are continually presented with brightly coloured toys, then their eyes become so accustomed to the obvious that they miss the play possibilities in the everyday things around them.
2 If they are presented with too many ready-made toys, their ability to imagine and improvise may be blunted.
3 If they are denied the satisfaction that imagination and improvisation afford, they may grow up to value things bought from shops above things they can make or improvise for themselves.
4 If you are pressured into buying countless toys to meet the supposed age and stage play needs of your children it will cost you a fortune – and may well impair your own sense of values.
5 If you put too much faith in 'educational toys' you may not see that *everything* that interests a child is 'educational' for lively living paves the way to learning for yet fuller living.

All this adds up to the fact that children don't need so many toys that they miss out the natural play objects in your home – for these have a particular significance. As far as possible, allow your child to explore everything that comes to hand, whilst removing precious or dangerous objects to a safe place, and make sure that cupboards and drawers within reach contain harmless dusters, brushes, cooking-tins, shoes, paper and string rather than bleach, aerosol cans, electric light bulbs, opened cartons of detergent, or cereals which may be harmless but are time-consuming to clear up.

Household contents are connected with the real business of living, and that is why no toys can be a substitute for this early finding out about the daily business of preparing food, washing up, cleaning, washing and ironing, decorating, gardening, personal hygiene and adornment – in short, homemaking.

If a child explores and plays with a plastic orange-squeezer until it is no longer interesting, then eventually sees you using one – and drinks the result of your efforts immediately – the connection between the plaything and the tool will eventually be made. After watching you many more times the apprentice may want to copy the master – and drink the result at once – before doing it again and offering it to another member of the family. Slowly the next connection between household tools and family life can be made and, just as important, sharp edges of distinction between work and play will be happily blurred for both of you – providing you don't always buy ready prepared food and drinks, thus undermining a great deal of basic learning.

I believe there is a connection between this early touching in the home and memories of homemaking that influence children in their own homemaking years later – it is not just what is done, but the atmosphere in which it is done. I also think that making the connections between cause and effect has its roots in the home too, not just in 'doing' but in relationships.

For all these reasons we should value childminders who supply this early experience for those parents unable to do so on a daily basis.

As long as all this home-based touching isn't missed out, then there are toys children greatly enjoy which will further encourage exploration and manipulation.

Are there traps for the unwary toy buyer?

1 Safety must come before all else. Be sure to buy toys

made by reputable firms. It is worth knowing that 95 per cent of British toy manufacturers belong to the British Toy Manufacturers Association and they make sure that their members' products are made to British Standard 3443. There are also government regulations which make it illegal to sell dangerous toys. But there is still the remaining 5 per cent and imported toys, some of which have lead paint, eyes on wires or spikes that are not safely anchored and protected, contaminated or dangerous stuffing, edges sharp enough to inflict a cut, parts which break and create a hazard as well as disappointment, removable parts that are small enough to be wedged in the throat, nose or ears, or manufacturing processes which involve dangerous or harmful chemicals.

2 Many toy firms try to give guidelines as to the age range for each toy. These can be misleading, so don't panic if your three-year-old can't 'do' a toy labelled 'For 2–3 years' or feel elated if your two-year-old 'does' a toy labelled 'For 3–4 years'. Children vary so much in their interests and aptitudes in these early years. Many won't even have discovered whether they are left- or right-handed, and may be a bit awkward with both.

3 Toys to avoid in the early destructive stages of play are those which can be broken or spoilt, for example little cars with tyres that can be prised off and dropped overboard. At this stage children sometimes don't even see the car as a car, but as an object to be handled and explored – and anything that is detachable is ripped off as the next stage of probing, pulling and twisting begins. The child is doing what is natural and helpful in many ways. You are likely to be upset because an expensive toy has been spoilt; and your distress will be bewildering since the motive behind the destruction wasn't 'naughty'.

If you can find some sturdy vinyl cars and other toys which are pliable and virtually indestructible for this stage, then everyone will be satisfied.

There is another reason for delaying the introduction of less sturdy models. If children become used to toys coming apart in their hands they may come to regard this as normal and not learn to treat them carefully; or may be so distressed that eventually they stop playing freely for fear of breakages.

If a child is going through a particularly destructive stage, it is particularly important that breakages are not the order of the day – to feel yourself to be the author of destruction can be frightening. There are plenty of toys designed to take the worst that children can do to them, and as an additional outlet there is clay and dough to bash and attack with the comforting discovery that they are exactly the same at the end as they were at the beginning, having absorbed the child's nervous and physical energy harmlessly.

4 It is natural for us to look at toys and say 'Isn't that lovely ... let's buy it!' when we mean 'I'd love that for myself, so I'm sure our child will love it.' It is difficult for us not to think of our children as smaller versions of ourselves. We have all seen proud fathers happily walking down the high street with a huge teddy bear or doll in their arms. They are saying 'I'm a dad! I've got a smashing kid and I'm taking home the biggest and best toy I can find. I can't wait to see the expression on that face when I hand this over.' And sometimes both child and parent are delighted with each other and the outsize toy. But sometimes it remains unplayed with because the size renders it inconvenient – imagine lugging around a doll two-thirds your own height! On the whole children need their toys to be physically comfortable to handle, and of a size that makes the child feel big and protective or big and domineering by turn.

What sort of toys do children need?

At last there is a guide book that will help you, *The Good Toy Guide*, produced by the Toy Libraries Association, Seabrook House, Darkes Lane, Potters Bar, Herts., EN6 2AB – a registered charity that has been testing toys independently for several years.

The TLA was founded by Jill Norris for her handicapped children and others in a similar position, who needed strong toys with good play value – and more of them than any one family could afford or store because their children's satisfaction was unpredictable, they could be very destructive and their concentration span varied from the obsessive to the very brief.

There are now several hundred of these toy-lending libraries all over the country and many more are planned. They try to meet the needs of as many children as possible in their area, but particularly the handicapped, whatever their disability. For eight years the Association's Advisory Panel has been testing the toys not only for their strength, safety and durability but for their play value. *The Good Toy Guide* lists several hundred recommended toys, all of which have been approved out of the thousands examined by the child care specialists of the TLA. They have also passed the test of constant use in a toy library.

The guide classifies the toys in seven sections, giving the name, description, manufacturer/supplier, measurements and guide price for each, and illustrations of some.

No one knows more than the TLA about toys, about their use by children and about the firms that make them. A copy of their guide can save money and disappointment.

What do parents need to know about toys?

The Good Toy Guide will help you to know about toys. The tricky bit is trying to combine children, toys and domestic harmony.

1 When children are lost in the world of their imagination they are as free as the birds, even within a confined space. Be careful how you break into their private world. Give them time to come down to earth before asking them to clear away for a meal or bed – ten minutes at least. And, if the game involves an elaborate floor layout of trains, stations, roads, garages and little playpeople all woven together in a master plan, perhaps you could be the one to adapt. A request to clear it away for lunch may leave you with a long afternoon and children gone flat and grumpy. A suggestion that perhaps they would like a transporter (you!) to bring provisions for the workforce may mean a quick improvisation of sandwiches, or large mugs of food to be hand-held on the floor – but also an after-noon of continuing play which will be a bonus for you all.

Be flexible, remembering that sustained creative play is now sadly rare. If you can encourage it you are to be congratulated, and both you and your children will certainly benefit in the long term.

2 Take children seriously, particularly if they set their heart on a particular toy and you sense that they *really* want it. It is no good giving such a child a crane and then being shocked if it is immediately used for scooping up buckets of real mud. You are not looking at a child spoiling a new and expensive toy but at a boss putting his new heavy plant to work. But like a good workman he should put his vehicles and tools away at the end of his labour.

3 It can't be said too often that children can only re-create what they have seen, and only then if they have seen it for long enough and often enough to take it in. Then as they reproduce what they have seen they begin to understand it as far as they are able to, and only then can they extend their play imaginatively.

There is no substitute for looking, listening, smelling and 'feeling' a new experience – be it a multi-storey car park, fire station, service bay, heel-bar, roadworks or a station. But it takes time, and someone who can point out *just* enough but not too much.

Try buying two platform tickets and taking a picnic with you for an hour on a station platform. Picnics give a sense of occasion. 'Let's have a sandwich each, then see what we can find to look at' – and off you go hunting with the child leading the way. Then 'Let's have another sandwich, then go hunting again.' If the timing has been right and the occasion happy, you may find an improvised platform being made at home – and because the episodes were separated by eating intervals they may stand out sufficiently clearly to be re-created one by one.

4 Children should put away their toys as a matter of course. I know it is much easier and quicker to put them to bed, then clear away yourself. Sometimes this has to be done, but as a general rule children shouldn't grow up with the idea that someone else will always clear up after them, someone else will look after their property and keep it safe, clean and mended, and someone else will make the home pleasant for them to come into.

Already you are laying down patterns in people who may one day be somebody's husband or wife!

Do children really need messy play?

All children need messy play. The idea may be abhorrent, but it is vital. Apart from the need to explore water, sand, mud, clay, paint and glue, being thoroughly dirty sometimes is important for children's mental health.

Children enjoy the different pleasures of dirtiness and cleanliness, and they need to know that we love them just as much dirty as clean.

We must be careful not to instil into them the false morality that dirtiness is naughty and cleanliness good. This just isn't true, though many people may find dirtiness repellent and cleanliness pleasing because of their upbringing. But that isn't morality, that is conditioning. Dirtiness and cleanliness are part of living, and should be experienced as freely as possible. What we have to learn is when each is appropriate and inappropriate, and if we have been brought up to feel anxious about mess, muddle and dirtiness and obsessive about cleanliness and tidiness our children may help to release us from some of our acquired inhibitions or false guilt.

If we are willing to learn it is amazing how children can help us to re-examine some of our set ways, and free us from old habits that we have never before questioned for ourselves.

The more imaginative toy manufacturers understand parents' anxieties, rational as well as irrational, and offer paints and adhesives that will wash out of clothing (some of the cheaper ones won't, so ask before you buy); plastic clay, if you can't buy or don't fancy natural clay; aprons with various degrees of 'cover-up' and water resistance; and more recently face paints which are harmless and great fun.

Once we accept that messy play is truly important it is a matter of unlearning certain stock remarks that we all use in one context or another.

If you change tidy clothes for play clothes, 'Look at you!' becomes 'It doesn't matter, they're only play clothes – they'll wash', 'Look at your hands!' becomes 'Let's wash those hands before they touch things.' And we can cut out the warning 'Now don't get dirty!' altogether. In appropriate clothes they *can* get dirty sometimes. But they don't need to be dirty all the time any more than they need to be clean all the time. As with their play, when they learn to move freely between reality and fantasy, so they need to move freely between dirtiness and cleanliness, knowing which is which and feeling at home with either.

But for this to happen they will need to sense your approval, for it is that which gives them 'permission' untroubled by anxiety or guilt. Your attitude to dirtiness is all-important – for once the TV advertisements have got it right, when Mum smiles at happy dirty youngsters and reaches for the packet that washes whitest.

Do I have to play with them?

It isn't necessary to play with children all the time; but, as with feeding, dressing, walking and all the other skills children are learning for the first time, they need us to initiate their early efforts, to leave them alone when all is going well, to be at hand to help when needed, to be a comforting presence when things go wrong, and a source of inspiration when staleness sets in.

Some parents play naturally, some feel bored or foolish, and some who think they don't like playing with their children are only very, very tired. If you really don't want to play, whatever the reason, then look at it again from your point of view. You don't want to play, but you probably don't want to be clambered over, whined at, or badgered with the constant moan 'I've got no one to play with!' either. If you could make one real effort for five *undivided* minutes three or four times each day you could find your child beginning to develop a pattern of play which will then give you a few minutes of unbroken peace and quiet.

Build towers of bricks for knocking over. Hand the bricks to the child for putting on top of each other – and let the builder be the demolisher. Build for yourself in your own way and for your own challenge and never mind if it is knocked over, for the idea will have taken seed that wonderful edifices can arise from bricks. Later, try building horizontally and eventually roads may carry little cars, and houses may appear along the way.

Construction kits of various kinds also acquire value in the child's eyes if parents will sit with them and just get them started. They are not ready to make anything specific in these early stages, only to get the general idea of what it is all about.

When they are confident about screwing, unscrewing, slotting, unslotting and pressing and pulling apart as the basic skills, then it can delight them if you create a monster model of your own occasionally. Not for them to copy, but just as an inspiration and as confirmation that parents play too.

Jigsaw puzzles can become a long-standing interest, but some children aren't interested, some find them very difficult, others take to them like ducks to water, while most can learn the art slowly – especially if you know whether it is more helpful to say 'Can you find a blue piece with white on it?' or 'We need a long thin piece with a bit sticking out in the middle' or 'Can you find the cat's tail?' Some children work by colour, some by shape, and some by picture sense – so offer different kinds of help in the learning stages.

What we need to remember is that play can't be used as a means to an end without it ceasing to be play. If you are playing, then play – don't be tempted to slip in any talk on colour, size, shape, vocabulary, number or general knowledge if it isn't *a natural part of friendly conversation*.

One teacher told a story against herself. 'I used to hang labels on furniture, and names on colours, and count things with her, until the day I gave her a poached egg on baked beans for dinner. She looked at them and said with a terrible sigh "I can see there's one egg, but do we *have* to count all the beans – couldn't I just eat them?" I told my husband – he'd been saying I was overdoing it – and next morning he came downstairs grinning all over his face with labels on him saying "Arm", "Head" and a big one saying "Daddy". It pulled me up. I've never done it again.'

So buy toys that children will love and use again and again in various ways and let the object in buying them be the child's pleasure and purpose. All else will come from that.

Chapter 18

We Never Stop Playing

Most of us become parents before we have stopped being children. What is sad is our twisting of the evidence into insult form. 'Stop being childish', 'Grow up!' 'Be your age', 'You're behaving like a child', we say. Precisely. And if we say these things in the heat of the moment we are also saying 'You don't understand the child in me who is being annoyed, provoked, hurt, frustrated and threatened by your behaviour – and neither do I.'

Some people retain a childlike curiosity, interest, wonder, self-esteem and capacity to labour and to love all their lives. Their answer to the old question at the end of each day, 'Hello, what have you been doing?', would be the one word:

'*Living!*'

Those less fortunate know that we are childish at times – but we still retain a child's gift for spontaneous play that would help us in our living if only we could avail ourselves of its healing, restorative and creative powers. All of us use different forms of play – imitative, imaginative, creative, compensatory, therapeutic and fantasy play to name but some – more than we realise or care to admit. But it would be even more rewarding if we recognised and acknowledged those times when spontaneous play comes to our aid, for that would help us towards a higher degree of awareness and self-knowledge.

I have talked about these forms of adult play with many people over the years and find there are areas of common experience it is reassuring and illuminating to share. When this sharing happens in a group there are always those who say 'Me too! Why didn't I see it before?' The answer to that question was put succinctly by Kahlil Gibran when he wrote 'No man can reveal to you aught but that which already lies half asleep in the dawning of your knowledge.'

Like children we have to repeat experiences again and

again and again before there is that wonderful moment of revelation when we suddenly 'see'.

These revelations can take us unawares and since they sometimes penetrate our self-protective armour there may be shock waves of guilt or remorse. Our false good image is cracked, yet it is in discarding these outer layers that we begin to find our true selves and our freedom. Each insight lifts some of the burden of self-deception, enriches our lives and make us more available to others.

With most children there seems to be a period when they become reticent about playing games of make-believe in front of others, though they may still share their private fantasies with a chosen one or two. My sister and I can recall such a period when we still shared a double bed but had outgrown the stage of scrabbling under the bedclothes to play 'houses'.

We used to go to bed with unwonted alacrity so we could carry on our 'thinking-parties'. Most are now forgotten, but we both remember planning feasts where 'first and afters' had no place – we conjured up cream doughnuts, baked beans on toast topped with sardines, ice creams in the tallest glasses in the world, sausages and mash, strawberries and cream, and everything else we loved.

Another fantasy was receiving an invitation to the Mansion House Christmas party, to which our enemy Petronella went every year because her father was one of the staff at the time. We decked ourselves out in washing-satin (having no knowledge of the genuine article) with alternating frills of palest pink and blue decorated with silvery bows and sashes – or we did until our friend Nora's big sister saw me colouring a clip-on dress for a cut-out cardboard doll in those colours and said 'You can't put pink and blue together, they're soppy.' After that we decked ourselves in scarlet, orange, purple and blue with trains and fox furs.

Then we discovered that these parties were fancy-dress affairs, so off we went to bed each night to dream up ever more elaborate costumes. We knew it was only wishful thinking, but on looking back we were consolidating knowledge we had absorbed through eating, drinking, wearing, doing, being, looking, listening and being read to. We were also giving free rein to our imaginations, and confidently and trustingly communicating our desires to each other. If only we all retained this ability! And if only parents weren't so quick to call out 'Stop talking, you two – be quiet and go to sleep'!

These thinking-parties only took place at night. There was something about nocturnal darkness and our state of relaxation that was conducive to shared intimacies. They never happened in the morning, not even dark winter mornings. The day was a time for planning and doing.

Later we shared less, perhaps because our fantasies began to centre on boys and we were aware of feelings that we didn't yet understand – and thinking-parties were based on rearranging and extending experiences that we knew very well indeed.

I can still remember the boy who was the centre of all these later thoughts and feelings. His name was Dick, he was tall and slim with red-gold wavy hair, and he rode a bicycle with panache. What I recall vividly is trying out various roles for myself and savouring the different kinds of satisfaction that each afforded. Sometimes he would be knocked off his bike by a lorry, or a pack of bullies, or an escaped bull, and I would rush to the rescue. There was nothing I couldn't do: climb a tree with his bleeding body on my back; carry out first aid with such breathtaking deftness that the crowd was spellbound; cradle him in my arms having dispatched others for help.

Sometimes the role was reversed and I would be the one to be pulled out of the path of a runaway bus; or lifted on to his crossbar and clasped tightly as he made a one-armed epic sprint to the hospital; or I would be unconscious (but not quite) as he anxiously bent over me.

The chief characteristic of all these fantasies and day-dreams was the pleasure they gave – and I was always pleased with myself. As far as I can recall I was never victimised (unless it was a mere prelude to being rescued) and never felt inadequate. The experience was not only pleasurable but of positive value as far as I can see.

In early imaginative play children try to find out what it is like to be someone else by copying what they do and say.

Perhaps the next stage is mental imaginative play, when we try to find out what it feels like to be various versions of ourselves. Surely this is valuable. It is sad when people say 'Well, that's the way I am and there's nothing I can do about it.' This may be so, but it may mean 'I've never even thought of being any other way, let alone explored it', or 'I'm like my mum (or dad) and that's good enough for me', or 'I feel so trapped and powerless that there is no escape.'

Maybe they didn't have thinking-parties – though this would surprise me. Or maybe the satisfied self of the fantasies was never able to be translated into action. If this is so, how important it is for children to be helped to feel powerful enough to be able to influence people and events sometimes. Another value that these fantasies may have is as a safe way of rehearsing for what is to come. I still find this form of mental rehearsal invaluable.

Being the first national adviser to the newly formed playgroup movement meant that there were endless first-times for all of us, for which none of us was really ready. Neither was there anyone to whom we could turn to say 'What did you do when . . . ?', 'How do you cope with . . . ?' or 'Did you find that . . . ?', because nobody, we thought, had worked with parents in quite our way before and we were finding that traditional assumptions were being turned upside down.

The first wave of learning was by trial and error, but eventually a body of experience was built up which enabled me to prepare myself to a certain extent by revising the old thinking-parties. Night after night I would replay the various versions of how assignment X might go. Only now I had to try to put myself in the places of those I knew, and also those about whom I had only been briefed – bearing in mind that the briefing could have been misinformed, biased or coloured by anxiety. Even this was not enough: having imagined the comments and questions that might come from each person involved I needed to answer them in spoken words, and this part of the rehearsal went on at odd moments during the day. It was about this time that friends and neighbours began to say 'You cut me dead the other day! You were miles away, talking to yourself!' I was indeed, in Devon or Manchester, Belfast or Jersey, or in a tiny village which was being torn asunder by the clash of conflicting interests.

The homework was never wasted for it meant I could rarely be taken by surprise, was flexible over the outcome, and relatively free of 'me' in order to watch and listen to what was happening in the hope of picking up sufficient clues to be able to help things forward. Without that mental rehearsal I think the failure rate would have been very much higher, and the wear and tear on my nervous system intolerable.

Another form of spontaneous play – in the sense of an action unconsciously aimed at relieving inner tension and restoring a feeling of well-being – is a degree of compulsive buying or eating, or both. Among children it is usually a matter of compulsive eating or taking.

With many women the buying goes like this. We are out shopping for household necessities and are more tired and limp than usual. Our heads may ache and our laden arms and weary legs certainly do. We may even feel faint or irrationally near to tears and dither instead of making quite simple decisions. We feel generally wretched and below par, and would give anything to wave a magic wand and find ourselves in the armchair at home with a pot of tea beside us and the shopping put away. So what do we do?

We gravitate to the nearest store and wander round the department where our particular weakness lies – cosmetics, gardening books or dresses. Most seem to make their way to the dress department, looking in a contradictory state of wanting and not-wanting to find something we like. Against our better judgement we may give in and try something on. If we don't like it or it doesn't fit, there is a wave of relief. This removes temptation and we can say to the hovering assistant 'No, I'm afraid it doesn't fit' and escape. If it fits we suffer the pull of temptation. A birthday present in advance? Spread it over two or three weeks' housekeeping and feed the family from the freezer stocks or cheap (but nourishing) food? Leave a deposit? If we give in, the chances are that the guilt outweighs the pleasure of possession. We may hide it from the family while we work out how and when to produce it, or say to an accompanying child 'Don't let's tell Daddy yet, let's keep it for a surprise!' But quite often it hangs in our wardrobe as a reproach.

So why do we do it? The answer goes something like this. You feel you've given and given to the family until there's nothing left to give. You're drained and empty. You want to go on giving but you can't until you are filled up again. It is unlikely that someone else will do this for you, because you have unwittingly created a pattern of anticipating and meeting other people's needs whilst keeping your own hidden. So you try to satisfy yourself in a childlike way by giving yourself a present or a treat.

I used to think this was a purely female trait until one day a man called out from the back of a hall 'Why do you assume it is only women who feel like that, and do that? We do it too!' And I suspect that we shall go on doing it until we learn to tell each other how we feel, and to ask for what we need from each other, or want to give each other.

I have a theory that one of the reasons for the success of Marks & Spencer, apart from the quality and price, is that their money-back guarantee takes the anxiety and guilt out of this kind of purchase. We can take the garment home, try it on after a good night's sleep, and know at once whether we shall or shan't keep it. It still takes courage to return the garment, for the state of mind in which it was bought makes it difficult to say simply 'I would like a refund on this, please.' Instead there are apt to be far-fetched excuses and mumbled apologies – followed by relief that the deed is done.

Compulsive eating at identifiable times is probably even more universal and is something I for one haven't outgrown. On the contrary, I give in to it on a short-term basis in the knowledge that when my feeling of equilibrium is restored I can – and do – rectify matters. There is the speaker's cycle which I share with many others: we can't eat much beforehand, coffee is 'out', and we all have our various physical reactions as the dreadful moment draws near – feeling sick, sweating, shivering, or switching off and feeling that we won't be able to switch on in time. After it is over we crave something that is excessively sweet and fills our mouths in a satisfying way. Two ounces of shelled walnuts, twelve ounces of tinned strawberries, two medium packets of potato crisps, or nine oranges would all supply roughly the same number of calories as my own preferred Mars bar – but none of them would do. Those of us who are similarly addicted – many of us incidentally not having a sweet tooth – know that the texture is as important as the sweetness.

I wonder how many children take things or gravitate to the biscuit tin as a way of saying 'I feel empty and I want to be filled up with attention – but if I can't get that I'll try biscuits, or sugar or jam'. I find more and more parallels between our spontaneous ways of trying to equalise pressure and children's. I'm not even alone in having once bought a hat as a bargain in a sale – an impossible pink fluted creation that looked like a lampshade, but did wonderful things for me after a longish stint of cooking and carrying pig swill, feeding the hens and ridding our home of ginger varnish. As soon as the family had departed for the office and school I put on my beautiful hat with no feeling of silliness at all. I wore it as I went about the household jobs and looked at it – and me in it – every time I passed a mirror. I felt 'pink' and feminine and graceful. I made the beds and washed up in a quite different way; prepared the evening meal as though I was serving teas in a stately home; floated downstairs, holding the countless things that need to be taken up or down as though they were a bouquet. I really *knew* how children feel when they become passionately attached to an item in the dressing-up box and want to wear it throughout their play until going-home time – and then say urgently 'Can I have it again tomorrow? You won't let anyone else have it, will you?' And I was glad my answer had always been 'No, I won't let anyone else have it, I will keep it for you.' There are times when adult 'fairness' and 'turns' are out of place, and deeper needs have to be met.

Another mother has told me that she remembers doing exactly the same thing with a distinctly moth-eaten fur cape she inherited from her mother, and several others have mentioned new scarves, earrings, headbands, wigs or frankly unsuitable garments that they couldn't resist – and from which they have had their private money's worth over and over again.

Childish or childlike? The latter I think, because the dressing up filled a need and created a feeling of harmony that was its own justification.

One of the most poignant discoveries has been learning how parents at breaking-point sometimes devise ways for diverting their pent-up, explosive feelings away from their children – much as children may attack a toy instead of the resented baby, and we say 'Let him, he's playing out his feelings safely.'

The pregnant mother of two young children, living in a first-floor flat in an area 'they call Dodge City, and say you need a gun and a passport to get in and out', said 'There are times when I get that wound up . . . and I know if I hit him I'd go too far. So I'll tell you what I do. I shut myself in my bedroom, kneel on the bed, and I punch the eiderdown and scream and scream and scream – until all the scream's gone out of me and then I'm perfectly all right. Sometimes I've pulled my hair until it comes out by the roots, and I'll be all right that way. But I'll tell you another thing I sometimes do: I bath, and wash my hair, and get all dressed up, and I just sit on the balcony – and that does the trick. Or I'll shut Gerald in his room and bang the door, and open it and bang it again – open, bang, open, bang, open, bang as hard as I can. The door frame comes loose in the wall, and afterwards I have to sweep up the plaster. But that way I'm all right. I know I won't hurt him.'

Another mother, living in a few small rooms in a run-down, vandalised London area said 'I've gone too far more than once and frightened myself. So now I lock them in their room and calm down by myself.' Another mother said 'I do that! When they're locked in I know they can't get into the street while I'm getting over it.' But the first one shook her head and said 'No, that's not why I do it. I lock them in so as I can't get at them.' No one in the group pointed out that if the key was in the lock she could still get at them – we knew that the turning of the key had symbolically turned off something inside and told her that both she and they were safe.

The childlike magic worked as surely as it does in children's play: 'You can't come in that way, that's the wall, there's the door', 'Here's your dinner, it's kippers and cream and a soup sandwich', 'You can't come in, the door's locked.'

Another mother in this group said 'I talk to myself. I shut myself in the bathroom or the loo, only the loo's got a seat so it's usually there. And I go over all the things I've just shouted at them, over and over again. And I find it alters a little bit each time, and when I've done I'm quite proud of the things I've said!'

In much the same way children try to restore their self-esteem. 'You know your best mug? Well, I didn't break it. I was just trying to bring you a drink, and when I was holding it very carefully the mat bumped my foot and then. . . . ' On and on the explanation goes until the culprit no longer feels like a careless, clumsy, inadequate child but a responsible person who had a bit of bad luck. If our self-esteem isn't strong we go on needing to boost ourselves in our own eyes whenever we feel we have let ourselves down. Thank goodness we can, and we shall go on needing to do so until someone does for us what we usually do for our children – take away the burden of guilt by our understanding, which lessens the likelihood of whatever it was happening again.

Something else I discovered was how often people quite consciously build their own personal playtime into each day. I first became aware of this in a row of terraced houses in the shadow of a car factory. There wasn't a tree or a blade of grass in sight, the front door opened straight on to the street, and the back yard was concreted to provide somewhere for the children to play out of doors. The young mother had been born in that street, served in the corner shop between leaving school and being married, and had then moved into another house in the same street. Rarely have I met a happier mother, and when I commented on this she said 'I'll let you into a secret. As soon as the *Mirror* comes in the morning I stuff in up my jumper under my left arm. Then whenever anything gets difficult I dig my elbow into my side until the paper crackles, and say to myself "Never mind, your time's coming, girl!" In the evening I put the children to bed, get my husband off to work – he works nights – wash up the tea things, and make up the fire. Then I fish my paper out, lie on my stomach on the hearthrug, and I read it from cover to cover.' She looked forward to that moment all day.

Another mother had found a different way. 'Life get's you down if you let it, so you have to find ways of keeping yourself up. Mine's jellytots. Bags of them, four or five bags a week. I save them up till the evening, and then I open one and eat the lot. I don't even throw the bag away, I hold on to it for several minutes. Everybody knows they're *mine*, not even the children ever touch them. They're Mummy's and that's that. Silly isn't it?' The group chorused 'No!' and a grandmother with arthritis, a troublesome hernia, poor eyesight, a daughter in a psychiatric hospital and two grandsons to bring up in a few rooms said 'I have a different time of the day that's mine. No one calls between half past nine and ten. I get a big bowl of water by the fire – we haven't got a bathroom – and I draw the curtains, and shut the door and fix it, and I have a good wash and take as long as I like. Well, you can't do it any other time. You've got to have a bit of privacy if you want to wash all over, haven't you? And the children are about all day, and my son-in-law has funny hours. But no one comes and disturbs me between half past nine and ten. And I can take a nice long time washing my feet.' The group was with her and we were moved by this, simply laying claim to the time to wash slowly, peacefully and in privacy as her personal enjoyment.

We have so much to learn from the intuitive wisdom of countless people who find their own daily way of relieving tension and restoring a sense of balance and well-being by giving themselves to the *now* of a spontaneous activity. When children do that, with the same result, we call it play.

Another valuable form of play that we frequently draw on, especially when faced with a new experience, is imitative play. I can see now how often I have done – and still do – this, but I can also remember the first time I became conscious of doing it.

For two or three years I had been working with local playgroup mothers for one evening a week, trying to devise an informal course that would help deepen their understanding of children and would also enrich their own lives –

not just as parents or wives but as people. Our experimental efforts were always interesting, often hilarious and sometimes painful, but we were all in it together and had lost our fear of being thought ignorant or foolish in each other's eyes. And then I was asked if I would be one of the tutors on an expanded day-long version of the course at the local college of further education. I felt flattered, elated and panic-stricken by turns – for the fall-back of 'Well, never mind, it's only an experiment' was no longer there.

When the day came I washed my hair, put on my best clothes, polished my shoes, and cleaned my handbag inside as well as out. Then for the first time my little A30 and I drove into the exalted surroundings of a staff car park. We were much too early and I sat looking at the imposing building, the like of which I had never taught in before. The make-or-break moment arrived – and suddenly I felt splendid. Remembering the elegant Peggy B. of my own college days I held my head high and made my way to the entrance. I savoured the moment of going to the staff rack to find my register, feeling absurdly important and elated. Having found it I glided along endless corridors, my handbag swinging from the crook of my elbow as I clasped the sacred register to my bosom.

I managed that bit to my complete satisfaction, and it carried me over the first few awkward minutes of wondering whether to start efficiently on time or wait for latecomers, whether to call the register formally or to fill it in as they arrived. Peggy B. had been courteous as well as formal, but I felt I was falling badly between two stools and my confidence began to waiver. I am still grateful she provided a model worthy to be remembered and used in my emergency, though it would have been no compliment to her had I become a carbon copy. But her example helped restore my shaken confidence as I found my feet and eventually my own style.

Playgroup people tell me they do this all the time. The new mother watches and copies the other mothers until she feels confident enough to be herself. Then she watches the rota mothers and tries to prepare herself for that role too. When she is a confident rota mother she may set her sights on being a helper – such a big step forward that the first morning often sees her in a new pair of jeans, dress or overall, partly to boost confidence but also to signify the importance to her of the transition from rota mother to 'staff'. Eventually helpers may become supervisors, and then they go through what I went through – pride, elation, excitement, but underlying it all the knowledge that this time the full weight of responsibility is theirs. People will still help, the atmosphere will still be happy and informal – but if they are not ready to assume full responsibility before sharing it they will have failed in their own eyes.

Again and again supervisors tell me of all the changes they were going to make as soon as they were in a position to do so, but that when the first day came their confidence was so shaky that they fell back on copying the old supervisor 'Just until I could find my feet'.

Since our first models are our parents the patterns they lay down are the ones we absorb most deeply and the ones which most affect the way we relate to our children. Sometimes we are not even aware of how much we are still copying our parents, but Samuel Butler was under no illusion when he wrote 'Some people seem compelled by unkind fate to parental servitude for life. There is no form of penal servitude much worse than this.'

Paradoxically, the happier childhood is the more difficult it can be to break the habits of thought, speech, attitude and action that bind us to the past when we should be growing towards independence. An older woman said to me recently 'On looking back I can see now that Mother was only really happy when we were all doing what she thought it would be nice for us to do, in the way she thought it should be done, and with people she approved of – but because she was so sweet and we loved her we simply didn't see it at the time. And neither, of course, did she.'

We need new models to inspire us throughout our lives, but perhaps never more than when we discover we have started to create a baby of our own. Not just 'a model', still less 'the right model', but a wide variety of people whose present experience is the same as ours; who may be reacting to it the same way or differently; who have the same or different attitudes to life in general; who offer us new ideas, ideals and insights; who may or may not appeal to us, but all of whom offer us alternative ways of coping with unfamiliar situations or the challenge of the moment.

When the first baby is born we are faced with yet newer experiences, and once again there is the need to meet others who are also going through it for the first time, together with those who are beyond this stage but still close enough to it to remember what it felt like. And so it goes on.

A phenomenon of our times is the upsurge of self-help groups which gather parents together at each new stage. The National Childbirth Trust, mother and toddler clubs and the Pre-school Playgroups Association are beginning to work more closely together to support parents in each area from pregnancy to school – and now there is the National Association for Primary Education for the support and enlightenment of parents and all those concerned with education at the next milestone in family life. These age divisions are crossed by other associations such as the National Association for the Welfare of Children in Hospital, Gingerbread for one-parent families, and Parents Anonymous for those who are desperate, while the National Childminding Association is part of the back-up service for those parents who need to go out to work, but still want their children to be brought up in a home and family setting. And all these groups are served by the rapidly expanding Toy Libraries Association and the many other statutory and voluntary services listed in local libraries.

Both the volunteers and paid workers in these associations work tirelessly – and that is the operative word. They have been caught up in an enterprise of their own choosing which interests and involves them; which stimulates, relaxes and restores a sense of balance; which consolidates skills and leads to the discovery and development of other abilities they didn't even know they possessed – and then uses those skills too.

In performing roles of this kind we are playing as children need to play – but sometimes can't because we divorce play from living, and haven't seen that children's needs are the same as ours.

We are all so concerned to help parents these days that we may have deflected them from what could be the real source of their insight and growth. We have come to see as out starting-point the parents who have produced the children – but perhaps it is time to acknowledge that it is the children who can, and often do, enable their grandparents' children to grow up.

When I started to write this book the first question people asked me was 'What's it about?' Then there was the predictable loss of interest when they discovered it wasn't a novel. The next question was 'Who's it for?' Then, when I replied 'Parents', they would say 'Ah! Telling them what to do, good for you' and change the subject.

No one can tell you what to do, and I shan't be offended if you don't remember a word I've written. But I hope that now and again you may have said to yourself 'I remember doing that' and that you may have allowed yourself to slip away on a tide of memories and feelings associated with them. I hope you may have been left with a stirring at the back of your mind, perhaps of feelings that are not yet quite in focus, flashes of recognition marked as unfinished business to be laid hold of later.

Above all, I hope that as you watch and listen to your own children and your own parents you will see that you are a part of them, they are a part of you – and that each link in the chain has to be forged anew.

Also available from Unwin Paperbacks

LIVING WITH A TODDLER
Brenda Crowe

One minute a toddler can be an angel, next moment a bawling, kicking, unreasoning tyrant. A source of great joy, and of frustration or despair. This book is designed to help parents when they often need help and advice most, and offers a wealth of ideas about a hundred and one aspects of living together – washing and dressing, meals, bedtime, outings, talking and listening, sharing the housework, helping each other – and how to deal with tantrums and sleeping and eating problems. She also gives a fascinating and revealing account of her own and other parents' experience of parenthood and discusses how to cope with the tiredness, loneliness and depression which can wear down even the most capable and cheerful parent.

ISBN 0 04 649015 9
£2.50

THE PLAYGROUP MOVEMENT
Brenda Crowe

This book was first written in 1973 as a report by
Brenda Crowe, the Pre-school Playgroups Association first National Adviser, and has been con-
siderably revised and updated for this new edition.
The playgroup movement is about parents providing for their own children and working together
to create better opportunities for them. This book
defines playgroups, examines their needs and
problems and traces the growth of the association to
meet the demands of a lively and demanding
movement.

ISBN 0 04 372039 0
£2.50

RUNNING A MOTHER AND TODDLER CLUB
Joyce Donoghue

Despite their rapidly increasing number, this is the first book about mother and toddler clubs, the popular meeting points for mothers and fathers and their under-3s. Addressed to parents starting or already running a club, it will also be invaluable for the voluntary workers, social and community workers, and health visitors who encourage these clubs from the sidelines. Pages of resources, key organisations, books, leaflets, films and topics for discussion, make this a handbook no one involved with mother and toddler clubs will want to be without.

ISBN 0 04 649030 2
£2.50

LEARNING THROUGH PLAY
Jean Marzollo and Janice Lloyd
Illustrated by Irene Trivas

This is a book to dip into when the children are bored or you are stumped for ideas, or to scour for inspiration when they are not around. It offers a delightful variety of ways to provide opportunities for encouraging children to develop their physical and mental skills through enjoyable, creative activities.

ISBN 0 04 649027 2
£2.95

SUPERTOT
A Parent's Guide to Toddlers
Jean Marzollo
Illustrated by Irene Trivas

A wonderful variety of games, activities and experiments to amuse one to three year olds and encourage them to learn about the world around them. Just a few of the many suggestions parents will find ideas and hints about are: games for indoors and out, building and making things, water, sand and clay play, car safety and car games, birthdays and parties.

ISBN 0 04 649026 4
£2.95

SUPERKIDS
Creative Learning Activities for Children 5–15
Jean Marzollo
Illustrated by Irene Trivas

This is a guide-book for active kids who like to *do* things: bake bread, plan parties, plant gardens, build birdhouses. Some projects, like publishing a neighbourhood newspaper, may be long-range. Others, like putting on an impromptu talent show, can be done spontaneously on a boring rainy day. Either way, ideal for kids who like to have fun.

ISBN 0 04 649028
£2.95

Also in Unwin Paperbacks

Learning Through Play *Jean Marzollo & Janice Lloyd*	£2.95	☐
Living with a Toddler *Brenda Crowe*	£2.50	☐
The Playgroup Movement *Brenda Crowe*	£2.50	☐
Running a Mother and Toddler Club *Joyce Donoghue*	£2.50	☐
Superkids *Jean Marzollo*	£2.95	☐
Supertot *Jean Marzollo*	£2.95	☐

All these books are available at your local bookshop or newsagent, or can be ordered direct by post. Just tick the titles you want and fill in the form below.

_____

Name ....

Address ....

....

....

Write to Unwin Cash Sales, PO Box 11, Falmouth, Cornwall TR10 9EN. Please enclose remittance to the value of the cover price plus:

UK: 50p for the first book plus 20p for the second book, thereafter 14p for each additional book ordered, to a maximum charge of £1.68.

BFPO and EIRE: 50p for the first book plus 20p for the second book and 14p for the next 7 books and thereafter 8p per book.

OVERSEAS: 85p for the first book plus 23p per copy for each additional book.

Unwin Paperbacks reserve the right to show new retail prices on covers, which may differ from those previously advertised in the text or elsewhere. Postage rates are also subject to revision.